the
anxiety workbook
for teens

activities to help you deal
with **anxiety & worry**

LISA M. SCHAB, LCSW

Instant Help Books
An Imprint of New Harbinger Publications, Inc.

Distributed in Canada by Raincoast Books

Copyright © 2008 by Lisa M. Schab
     Instant Help Books
     An Imprint of New Harbinger Publications, Inc.
     5674 Shattuck Avenue
     Oakland, CA 94609
     www.newharbinger.com

Cover Design by Amy Shoup

Illustrated by Julie Olson

All Rights Reserved

Printed in the United States of America

Library of Congress Cataloging-in-Publication Data

Schab, Lisa M.
  The anxiety workbook for teens / by Lisa M. Schab.
    p. cm.
  Includes bibliographical references and index.
  ISBN-10: 1-57224-603-0 (pbk. : alk. paper)
  ISBN-13: 978-1-57224-603-4 (pbk. : alk. paper) 1. Anxiety in adolescence--Problems, exercises, etc. I. Title.
BF724.3.A57S33 2008
155.5'1246--dc22

         2008002238

17 16 15

25 24 23 22 21 20 19 18

contents

Dear Reader,

Welcome to *The Anxiety Workbook for Teens*. If you have been given this book, it is probably because you are experiencing anxiety in your life in some way and you are hoping to either get rid of it or learn how to handle it.

If you are experiencing anxiety, you are normal. There is no one who doesn't feel anxious at some time. It is even more common to feel anxious during adolescence, because so many changes are taking place in your body, your mind, and your emotions.

Anxiety is a common and very treatable condition. Working through the activities in this book will give you many ideas on how to both prevent and handle your anxiety. Some of the activities may seem unusual at first. You may be asked to try doing things that are very new to you. Even if the suggestions seem really different from what you are used to, I encourage you to give them a try. The idea that seems the strangest may turn out to be the one that helps the most.

You will also find that, while some activities work very well for you, others don't help at all. That is normal, too. You are a unique person, and you will have to discover the activities that work the best for you. Please feel free to talk with a counselor or other adult about altering the activities in some way if you find a better method than is suggested here. Be creative, and trust your intuition about what feels good to you and what doesn't.

As you complete the exercises, there will be times when you are asked to draw. Many people get intimidated when they read the word "draw." They think that they aren't good at art and might be embarrassed by their attempts. Please be aware that there are no right or wrong ways to draw your answers. The purpose of drawing in this book is only to lead you to a better understanding of yourself and your anxiety.

There is one thing that the activities have in common: they won't help if you do them just once. They are tools, intended for you to carry with you and use over and over throughout your life. The more you practice using them, the better you will become at managing anxiety.

Try to be patient with yourself as you take steps along your path to peacefulness. It may take time to find your answers, but be assured that they are there! You will find them as long as you stay on the path.

Lisa M. Schab, LCSW

you need to know

Anxiety is a common feeling usually described as "uneasiness" or "apprehension." At one time or another, everyone experiences anxiety. It is highly treatable and manageable.

The feeling of anxiety has been described with many different words. Here are some of them:

stress	edginess	apprehension	the jitters
worry	jumpiness	nervousness	the shakes
fear	butterflies	uneasiness	freaking out
panic	disquiet	agitation	angst

While everyone experiences anxiety, some of us feel it more often, some more deeply, some less frequently, and some less intensely. Your own experience of anxiety will depend on:

1. Genetics—how your parents, grandparents, and ancestors experienced anxiety

2. Brain chemistry—the type, amount, and movement of the chemicals working in your brain

3. Life events—the situations you are faced with in your life

4. Personality—how you look at and interpret things that happen to you

Genetics, brain chemistry, and life events are factors that you have little or no control over. Your personality, or the way you perceive and handle life events, is something you have a great deal of control over—probably more than you realize. For that reason, most of the activities in this book will focus on working with your personality, helping you to understand the way you look at and respond to life and suggesting ways to do it that will help you to lower your anxiety level.

activity 1 ✳ about anxiety

directions

Your closest ancestors are your mother, father, grandparents, and great-grandparents on both sides of your family. In person, by phone, or in writing, interview as many of these people as you can. Ask them the following questions and record their answers on separate sheets of paper.

1. Which of the following words would you use to describe anxiety? (Read or show them the list on the preceding page.)

2. Would you describe yourself as a highly anxious, moderately anxious, or rarely anxious person, and why?

3. Explain how you experience the feeling of anxiety in your body, mind, and emotions.

4. Explain what you do to manage anxiety when you feel it.

5. Describe how any or all of your responses may have changed over the course of your life.

Now ask yourself the same questions and record your answers here:

1. _____

_____

2. _____

_____

3. _____

_____

4. _____

_____

5. _____

_____

more to do

Look back over the answers to your relatives' interview questions. Describe any patterns you see in the answers.

_____

_____

_____

_____

_____

How do your relatives' answers compare to your answers?

_____

_____

_____

_____

What, if anything, do you better understand about yourself in relation to anxiety by having learned about your relatives?

_____

_____

_____

_____

2 the chemistry of anxiety

for you to know

Our bodies respond to anxious thoughts by emitting stress hormones. This built-in biological reaction is called the fight-or-flight response.

In prehistoric times, humans faced challenges different from those they face today. For example, a common challenge for prehistoric man may have been to walk outside his cave in the morning and find himself face-to-face with a huge, hungry lion.

Human bodies are miraculous creations that are programmed to survive. When confronted with a threat such as a lion, the brain would send the signal, "Threat!" and the body would respond by shooting hormones, such as adrenaline, into the bloodstream at lightning speed. That made the body immediately stronger and faster so the human could either wrestle the lion (fight) or run away very fast (flight). When humans either fought or ran away, the physical exertion would disperse the hormones, and the body chemistry would quickly return to normal.

In today's world, our bodies still release stress hormones when we are faced with a threat. The chemical release raises our blood sugar, heart rate, blood pressure, and pulse; slows our digestion; dilates our pupils; and causes us to breathe more shallowly. While these changes prepare us for fast action, we don't usually take it, so our hormones don't disperse. You may become anxious when you look at the history test your teacher has just handed you and realize you don't know any of the answers, but you are not likely to respond by fighting with the history teacher or running from the classroom. As you sit at your desk "stewing," the anxiety just continues to build. Built-up anxiety makes us vulnerable to emotional and physical problems. To stay healthy, we have to find ways to avoid or disperse those chemicals.

directions

In the space below, draw a picture of yourself standing at the door of your bedroom first thing in the morning. Outside your bedroom door, draw or write all of the challenges you are confronted with on an average day that might cause your body to emit stress chemicals.

more to do

Look at your picture of daily challenges. Write them here in the order of how anxious they make you feel. Write those that make you feel most anxious first and those that make you feel least anxious last.

_____

_____

_____

_____

Describe the physical symptoms you experience when you feel anxious about any of these things.

_____

_____

_____

_____

_____

Our bodies emit flight-or-flight response chemicals whether the threat we perceive is internal, external, real, or imagined. Which challenges in your picture are:

internal?	external?	real?	imagined?
_____	_____	_____	_____
_____	_____	_____	_____
_____	_____	_____	_____
_____	_____	_____	_____

Do you react by physically fighting or physically running away from any of these threats?

_____

_____

_____

Describe how you react if you don't fight or run away.

_____

_____

_____

Describe any realistic ideas you have about how you could release the buildup of stress hormones from your body.

_____

_____

_____

_____

3   peace is already within you

you need to know

Many people think that peace is something we have to look for outside of ourselves or work very hard to create within ourselves. Actually, peace is a natural state of being that is already within us; it is just hidden by all of the stress and tension we take in and focus on.

When the renowned fourteenth-century artist Michelangelo was asked how he created the exquisite and powerful statue of David from a solid piece of marble, he replied that David was already in the stone; he simply chipped away the excess. Like the statue of David, your peace is already within you. You simply need to unearth it by peeling off the layers of anxiety that are covering it up.

You cover up your peace every time you think of, or dwell on, a stressful thought. The thought does not destroy your peace, but it can cause you to forget it if you continue to dwell on the anxiety.

directions

Shade in the pictures of the floating clouds below with a pale blue crayon or another light color. The clouds represent your natural state of peace. Then take a few minutes to sit quietly, breathe slowly, look at those peaceful clouds, and feel that deep relaxation within you.

Next, using a darker color, cover up the clouds by writing the names of people, situations, or things that make up the anxiety in your life. Write as many stressful things as you can think of.

more to do

When you looked at the shaded clouds, were you able to feel the peacefulness they represented? If you were, write about what that was like. If not, tell what you think prevented you from feeling it.

_____

_____

_____

_____

Tell what it was like for you to cover up the peaceful clouds with stressful thoughts and words.

_____

_____

_____

_____

Think about how you cover up your own natural state of relaxation when you choose to dwell on anxious thoughts. Describe a time when you remember feeling calm but lost sight of that feeling when you began to think anxious thoughts.

_____

_____

_____

_____

As you go through the rest of the week, be aware of the times that you cover up your natural state of relaxation with tension.

prevention and intervention 4

for you to know

There are two ways to work on managing anxiety. The first is by practicing prevention, which means that you spend time doing relaxation techniques on a regular basis to keep your everyday anxiety at a low level. The second is by practicing intervention: at the time you feel your anxiety level rising, you perform a relaxation technique to help you calm down and manage the current situation.

Some people don't understand why they should practice relaxation techniques *before* they are feeling anxious. To help you understand why it is a good idea, think about your teeth. Do you wait until you have a cavity to start brushing your teeth? Most of us brush our teeth every day because it helps prevent cavities from forming. It is the same with anxiety. If you practice relaxation techniques every day, you can better prevent anxiety from forming.

Some of the relaxation techniques you will learn in this book are best used for prevention, before you feel anxiety, and some are best used for intervention, at the time you feel anxiety. Many of the techniques can be used at both times. It is important to remember that the more you practice the techniques as prevention, the better you will be able to use them for intervention.

directions

Put a "P" next to the phrases that describe activities done as prevention (before a situation or event) and an "I" next to the phrases that describe activities done as intervention (at the time of a situation or event).

_____ Studying for a test

_____ Recalling information at the time of a test

_____ Eating a variety of healthy foods daily

_____ Drinking juice when you have a cold

_____ Slamming on your brakes to avoid an accident

_____ Driving at the speed limit

_____ Setting your soda can on a coaster

_____ Cleaning soda rings off the coffee table

_____ Washing your face on a daily basis

_____ Applying acne cover-up when your face breaks out

_____ Saving part of your allowance or paycheck each week

_____ Asking your parents for a loan when you need extra money

_____ Putting gas in your car when the gauge reads empty

_____ Putting gas in your car when the gauge reads one-quarter full

_____ Bringing a granola bar in your backpack in case you get hungry

_____ Buying a granola bar at a vending machine when you get hungry

_____ Paying your cell phone bill by the due date

_____ Paying your cell phone bill when your service gets turned off

_____ Wearing a wristguard when you go bowling

_____ Doing wrist-strengthening exercises twice a week

more to do

Describe three activities you have done in the past week that could be considered prevention.

1. _____

2. _____

3. _____

Describe three activities you have done in the past week that could be considered intervention.

1. _____

2. _____

3. _____

Describe a situation in which your intervention would have been better if you had also practiced prevention.

_____

_____

_____

Describe any activities you already do to prevent your anxiety level from getting too high.

_____

_____

_____

Describe what you usually do to help yourself when your anxiety level gets very high.

_____

_____

_____

5 how you experience anxiety

for you to know

The way you experience anxiety may be different from the way your friend or relative experiences it. Increasing your awareness of how you experience anxiety can help you to manage it.

Marcus, Danielle, and Emily all experience "test anxiety." Whenever they have a big test coming up in school, they start to feel very anxious. Even though all three of them have this reaction, they all experience anxiety in different ways.

Marcus always has a hard time sleeping for a couple of nights before a test. He finds it hard to fall asleep because his mind is racing with thoughts about the subject he has been studying, the facts he is trying to memorize, what he thinks the essay questions will be, whether he studied enough, and whether he studied the right materials. Even when he finally falls asleep, he wakes up frequently and often dreams about being late for class on the day of the test or not knowing any of the answers.

Danielle has no trouble sleeping before a test, but she tends to get "knots" in her stomach. She doesn't have much of an appetite because the muscles in her stomach area feel very tight, which prevents her from feeling hunger pangs. She has to force herself to eat tiny meals or snacks even though she's not hungry, because if she doesn't eat she gets light-headed.

Emily experiences test anxiety as an overall nervousness. She finds it hard to concentrate and has a constant sense of uneasiness. She tends to get lost in her thoughts and feels jumpy or antsy. She notices that her heart seems to beat a little faster and her breathing is shallower during the morning of a test.

Recognizing their anxiety helps Marcus, Danielle, and Emily know what is happening when they feel these symptoms. They realize that they are nervous about the upcoming test. The earlier they notice their reactions, the sooner they can practice relaxation techniques to help alleviate these symptoms and keep them from getting worse. If they don't take care of themselves early enough, Marcus might fall asleep during the test, Danielle would have trouble thinking of the answers because her brain isn't getting enough nutrition, and Emily could be too distracted to be able to complete the test in the time allowed.

directions

Think about the ways you experience anxiety. In the picture below, make notes or marks on the parts of the body where you feel anxiety symptoms. Use different colors, textures, lines, or shading to help express your feelings more precisely.

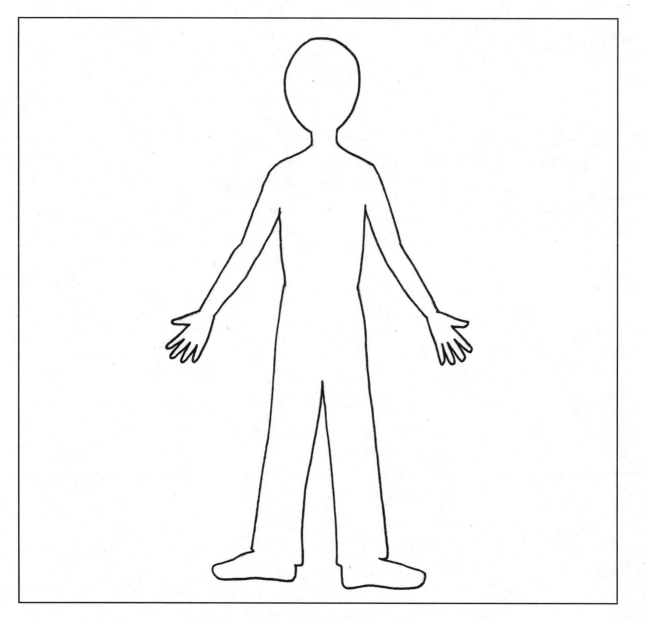

more to do

Were you able to remember what anxiety feels like for you? If not, pay attention to how you experience anxiety over the next week, and then repeat this exercise when you have more information about yourself.

What was it like trying to show your feelings in the picture?

_____

_____

_____

When you look back at your body outline again, what are your thoughts and feelings about how you experience anxiety?

_____

_____

_____

According to the picture, where and how do you feel anxiety the most?

_____

_____

_____

How do you think noticing your symptoms when they first begin might be helpful for you?

_____

_____

_____

6 your anxiety patterns

for you to know

When you understand the thoughts and situations that trigger feelings of anxiety within you, you can better help yourself to prevent and manage it. A behavior log can help you learn about your anxiety patterns.

Alex used to describe himself as a nervous person. He felt like he was more anxious than most people, and that made him very shy. He was always afraid he would say or do something when he was nervous that would make him look stupid or make people laugh at him. He thought he always had to be a little guarded to keep from doing or saying something embarrassing. There were only a couple of people with whom he felt comfortable enough to be himself. Alex would have liked to be able to relax enough to meet more people, but he didn't know how.

His counselor wasn't sure that Alex's nervousness was as much of a problem as Alex felt it was. She asked him to try keeping a behavior log to make him aware of the times and situations when he experienced anxiety. A copy of part of Alex's log is shown on the next page. Alex was surprised to realize that he was highly anxious only in certain situations with certain people—usually peers whom he perceived as smarter than himself. He realized that there were also many times when he felt confident, mainly with adults, but also with peers that he felt were at his intellectual level. This new knowledge helped give him the courage to better handle the times he did feel anxiety and to take small risks to meet new people.

Alex's Behavior Log

Day	Time	Situation	What I'm Thinking	My Anxiety Level
Saturday	6 p.m.	Meeting my parents' friends who came to our house. I have a 15-minute conversation with them.	These people are nice and easy to talk to.	low
Sunday	2 p.m.	At a baseball game with my dad. Run into some kids I know from school. Talk for 5 minutes.	These kids are in Student Council Club with me. I'm surprised they came over to say hi. Maybe they like me.	medium
Monday	4 p.m.	Watching my little brother after school. Helping him and his friends practice batting.	These kids are cute. I know a lot more than they do.	low
Tuesday	11 a.m.	Working on group project in chemistry class.	Everyone understands this stuff better than I do. They probably think I'm stupid.	high
Thursday	3 p.m.	Sitting on the bus with Nathan, the smartest kid in the school.	If I open my mouth and say anything, I'll sound dumb. I better just sit here and stare out the window.	high
Friday	7 p.m.	Having pizza at David's house.	I'm glad David is my best friend. He's fun, and we like the same things.	low

directions

The behavior log on the next page gives you a place to record observations about the times you feel anxious. Make as many copies as you need and use them to record information about your feelings of anxiety for at least one week.

My Behavior Log

Name _____ Week of _____

Day	Time	Situation	What I'm Thinking	My Anxiety Level

more to do

After you have filled out the behavior log for a week, answer the following questions:

What was it like to pay attention to your feelings of anxiety by keeping this log?

_____

_____

_____

Did keeping the log tend to make you more or less anxious? Why?

_____

_____

_____

Look back over your log. Describe any patterns you notice over time.

_____

_____

_____

Describe any new information you learned about yourself from keeping this log.

_____

_____

_____

How can you use this log to help you understand and manage your feelings of anxiety?

_____

_____

_____

7 having an awesome attitude

for you to know

Do you think? If the answer to that question is yes, then you already know how to use an awesome anxiety-management tool. Your thoughts create your experience of life. Your attitude, or the way you think about things, is one of the most powerful tools you have to help you prevent and manage feelings of anxiety. And since you are the only one who controls your thoughts, at every moment you have the ability to create a peaceful experience or an anxious experience for yourself.

Tristan and Jon were training for their school's big cross-country meet. They decided to meet at the field house at noon on Saturday to run a ten-mile course through the surrounding neighborhoods. Saturday turned out to be the hottest, most humid day of the summer. The boys laid out their course and then started off. About one-third of the way through, both boys were really feeling the heat, but they didn't want to stop because they needed the training. They kept running, getting hotter and thirstier with every step. By the time they were two-thirds of the way through, all that either of them could think about was a cool drink of water. When they finally hit the last stretch, they were hotter than ever and their clothes were drenched with sweat. Upon reaching the school, they both ran straight for the drinking fountain, only to find that it wasn't working. There was no drinking water at all except for a half-full water bottle sitting next to the fountain. Tristan had left it there before they started their run. Both boys looked at the same water bottle, and both had different reactions.

Tristan said, "Oh man! I am so glad I left this water bottle here! It's just half full, but that's better than nothing! Gee, are we lucky to have this!" Tristan's attitude made him feel peaceful.

Jon looked at the very same water bottle and said, "Oh no! I can't believe this is all we have! This is terrible! I could drink ten full bottles myself, and all we have is a half of one!" Jon's attitude made him feel anxious.

Each boy was in the same situation, but each experienced it very differently having nothing to do with the situation itself. Their experiences came from within each of them—from their attitudes.

activity 7 * having an awesome attitude

directions

In each pair of pictures below, two young people are in the same situation, but you can tell by the looks on their faces that they are experiencing it differently. Under the pictures, write what each person might be thinking to cause their individual feelings.

_____

_____

_____

_____

_____

_____

more to do

Describe a recent situation in which you experienced anxiety.

_____

_____

Tell what you were thinking that caused this anxiety.

_____

What could you have thought to make the experience a peaceful one instead?

_____

_____

Describe a recent situation in which you felt peaceful.

_____

_____

Tell what you were thinking that caused you to feel peaceful.

_____

What could you have thought that would have made the experience an anxious one instead?

_____

_____

Read over the two situations you just wrote about. If possible, share them with another person. Think and talk about the awesome power of your attitude to affect how you experience life.

As you go through the upcoming days, notice how your attitude about anything that happens affects your anxiety level.

8 worrying is worthless

for you to know

It is common for people to worry about things that they feel anxious about. However, all the time and energy that is spent in worry is actually wasted. When you try to alleviate anxiety by worrying, all you do is make the anxiety grow stronger.

Most people don't realize why they worry. They think worrying is something that just happens. Or they say they "have to" worry about something. That is not true, of course. Usually we begin to worry because we feel anxious about a situation and we want to do something to try to prevent a negative outcome. If it is a situation that we have little or no control over, there is not much we can do. Not being able to do anything brings up feelings of helplessness, which trigger worry. Worrying is something we can do. When we worry, we may feel we are doing something to try to control the situation.

People have worried about things for centuries, but it has never once had a positive effect on the outcome of a situation. If there were any possible way that worrying would help you to relieve anxiety, there would be an exercise in this book teaching you how to worry and suggesting that you practice it diligently as both prevention and intervention.

What worrying does do is to drain you, both emotionally and physically. That makes your situation worse because you have less energy to handle whatever it is that is going on. Then your anxiety level goes up again because you feel even more helpless.

directions

Rate your present anxiety level on the scale below.

0	1	2	3	4	5	6	7	8	9	10
Completely peaceful					Moderately anxious					Highly anxious

Now think of a current situation that is bringing up feelings of anxiety for you. Set a timer for five minutes or keep an eye on a clock. Spend the next five minutes worrying about this situation. Use all of your skills and past experience in worrying to worry as hard as you can. Think about all the negative ways this situation could turn out. Put as much emotional and physical energy as you can into worrying. Imagine you will be graded on how well you can worry, and try to worry hard enough to get an A+.

After the five minutes is up, rate your anxiety level again on the scale below.

0	1	2	3	4	5	6	7	8	9	10
Completely peaceful					Moderately anxious					Highly anxious

more to do

What was it like to spend five minutes purposely worrying hard about something?

_____

_____

_____

How did this purposeful worrying affect your anxiety level?

_____

_____

_____

What happens to your body and your mind when you worry so hard?

_____

_____

_____

Describe any way that the worrying you just did will have a positive effect on the outcome of the situation.

_____

_____

_____

Describe something you could do instead of worrying that would be more productive or would help you feel better.

_____

_____

_____

all-or-nothing thinking 9

9

for you to know

All-or-nothing thinking is the tendency to judge things in extreme or "black-and-white" categories. It is irrational, because in reality things are never completely one way or the other. Judging yourself in this way raises your anxiety level. You are always afraid that if you don't achieve perfection (one extreme) you will be a complete failure (the other extreme).

Max was usually a straight-A student. He thought of himself as very intelligent. But if he received a B on a test or homework paper, he would think, "Now I'm a total failure." He also thought he had great leadership skills, but when he lost the election for class vice president, he told himself, "Now I'm a zero." When Max headed the committee for the class picnic and they ran out of hamburger rolls, Max said, "I'm worthless as a planner."

This kind of all-or-nothing thinking caused Max to feel anxious before he took on any task because he was always afraid of not being able to achieve perfection (one extreme) and thus having to label himself as a failure (the other extreme).

directions

Nothing in life is completely one extreme (black) or the other extreme (white). Real people and situations have different mixes of negative and positive. Reality exists in the gray area between black and white.

The boxes below show that there is a large gray area between the extremes of black and white. For each category listed, put a mark to show where your own realistic experience lies.

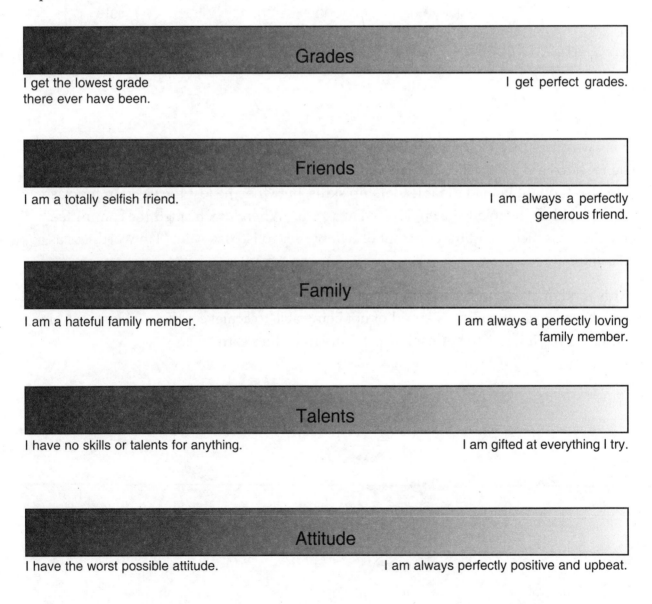

Grades

I get the lowest grade there ever have been.

I get perfect grades.

Friends

I am a totally selfish friend.

I am always a perfectly generous friend.

Family

I am a hateful family member.

I am always a perfectly loving family member.

Talents

I have no skills or talents for anything.

I am gifted at everything I try.

Attitude

I have the worst possible attitude.

I am always perfectly positive and upbeat.

more to do

Describe what it felt like to rate your gray areas in these categories.

_____

_____

_____

In which categories was it hardest to rate yourself in the gray area rather than the black or white extremes? Why did you choose those categories?

_____

_____

_____

What do you think might be hard about giving up all-or-nothing thinking and seeing things more realistically?

_____

_____

_____

Rewrite the all-or-nothing statements that Max told himself, replacing them with realistic gray-area statements:

"Now I'm a total failure."   _____

"Now I'm a zero."   _____

"I'm worthless as a planner."   _____

activity 9 ✳ all-or-nothing thinking

Write three examples of all-or-nothing statements you have made about yourself. Then rewrite them, replacing them with realistic gray-area statements.

1. _____

2. _____

3. _____

1. _____

2. _____

3. _____

Tell which of the above statements makes you feel the most anxious, and why.

_____

_____

_____

overgeneralizing 10

> ## for you to know
>
> When people overgeneralize, they assume that because they had one negative experience in the past, they will always have the same negative experience in the future—even though there is no evidence for that. This assumption raises their anxiety level whenever they encounter a situation that has been negative, even just once, in the past. People who overgeneralize often use the words "always," "never," "no one," "everyone," "all," and "none."

When Lauren asked a boy she liked to the school dance, he said no. She thought, "No one will ever want to date me; I'm always being rejected." She began to feel anxious anytime she was with a boy she liked.

When Lauren dropped her lunch tray in the school cafeteria, which had never happened before, she told herself, "It figures; I'm such a klutz. I'm always causing accidents." Lauren became nervous about dropping food and dishes even when she was at home clearing the kitchen table.

When Lauren babysat for the first time, the baby had an earache and wouldn't stop crying. Lauren told herself, "I'll never be good with children; I'll make a terrible mother." When she was called to babysit again, she got nervous just thinking about it and turned the job down.

These kinds of overgeneralized thoughts caused Lauren's anxiety level to go up in any situation where her past experience hadn't been perfect.

activity 10 ✳ overgeneralizing

directions

The kids in the pictures below are having negative experiences. Next to each picture, write an overgeneralizing statement they might make about their situation that would raise their anxiety level. Use the words "always," "never," "no one," "everyone," "all," or "none." Then, write a more realistic statement that could lower their anxiety level.

1a. _____

_____

_____

1b. _____

_____

_____

2a. _____

_____

_____

2b. _____

_____

_____

3a. _____

_____

_____

3b. _____

_____

_____

more to do

For the next few days, keep a record here of any statements you make that use the words "always," "never," "no one," "everyone," "all," and "none." Describe the situation you were in when you made each statement.

_____

_____

_____

_____

Look back at what you have written. Describe any patterns you notice in the subject areas or situations that you overgeneralize about.

_____

_____

_____

_____

Now rewrite the statements, replacing the overgeneralizing words with more accurate words.

_____

_____

_____

_____

Read both groups of sentences aloud to yourself, paying attention to your anxiety level as you read them. Notice which statements make you feel more anxious.

11 "should" statements

for you to know

Using the word "should" is appropriate when there is something we need to do or a way we need to act in order to be responsible or courteous. But "shoulds" can get out of control and raise your anxiety level when they are unrealistic or unimportant.

Brandon was frequently anxious because so many of his thoughts used the word "should." When he was riding the bus to school, he thought, "I should be using this time to study." When he was at a chess club meeting, he thought, "I should be in a sport instead. It would be so much cooler." When his bike chain broke and he didn't know how to fix it, he thought, "I should be more competent and know how to fix this myself." When he failed a math test because he had gone to a baseball game instead of learning the material, he thought, "I should have studied harder for this test."

Brandon's counselor helped him to think more carefully about his "should" statements to see how realistic or important they were. Here is what he discovered about his thoughts:

- "I should be using this time to study."
  I spend several hours on homework each night. My grades are good. Realistically, if I spend every waking moment studying, I will burn out quickly. It is probably healthier to use my time on the bus as a mental break.

- "I should be in a sport instead. It would be so much cooler."
  Some kids think that sports are cooler than chess. But I don't really like sports and I do like chess. I'm not that good at sports and I'm great at chess. I would rather have fun in the chess club than be miserable in sports just because of what some kids think. My real friends like me no matter what.

- "I should be more competent and know how to fix this myself."
  When I can't do something, I tend to get down on myself. But I am good at a lot of things. I can't know how to do everything. Fixing my bike is something I can just get help with.

- "I should have studied harder for this test."
  This thought is very realistic. I didn't use my time wisely, and I could have done much better if I had taken more time to learn the material.

activity 11 ✳ "should" statements

directions

Make a list of your own "should" statements. After each one, write more detail about how realistic or important they are.

_____

_____

_____

_____

_____

_____

_____

_____

_____

_____

_____

_____

_____

_____

more to do

Tell how your "should" statements are similar to or different from Brandon's.

_____

_____

_____

_____

Tell where most of your "should" statements originated and why you think that is so.

_____

_____

_____

_____

Tell which "should" statement raises your anxiety level the most and why.

_____

_____

_____

_____

Go back to your list and cross out any "should" statements that are unrealistic or unimportant. Put a star next to the statements that are realistic or important. Choose one statement to work on changing, and make a conscious effort to do it in the coming week.

12 thought stopping

for you to know

Thought stopping is a technique that can help you let go of thoughts that cause you to feel anxious and change them to thoughts that help you feel peaceful.

Kaitlyn worried about her father. In his new job, he had to travel a lot and he was flying in airplanes twice as often as he used to. Kaitlyn had always been a little afraid of flying, and now she found herself waking up in the middle of the night thinking about her dad's safety. Her thoughts raised her anxiety level, and then she had a hard time going back to sleep. She also found herself thinking anxious thoughts about her dad when she was supposed to be concentrating on homework, in the middle of a conversation with a friend, or watching TV. Her anxious thoughts were following her everywhere and interfering in her life.

One night, Kaitlyn read a magazine article about managing anxiety, which gave these instructions for stopping anxiety-producing thoughts:

Kaitlyn tried the thought-stopping technique and found that after some practice, it began to help her. Whenever she found herself having an anxious thought about her dad, she immediately told herself to STOP. Then she consciously replaced her anxious thought with a thought about walking her dog on the beach in the summer, which made her relax and smile. When she stopped her anxious thoughts, her anxious feelings stopped too.

Five Steps for Thought Stopping

1. Notice that you are having a thought that causes anxiety.

2. Choose a way to immediately and forcefully tell yourself to STOP this thought. Some ideas include saying "Stop!" out loud or in your mind; picturing a bright red stop sign; picturing yourself pushing your arm out in front of you with your hand in a "halt" position; keeping a light rubber band around your wrist and snapping it gently; giving your head a quick shake as if you were physically shaking off the thought.

3. Consciously exchange the anxious thought for a peaceful thought. You can plan your peaceful thought ahead of time so it's ready immediately.

4. Say your peaceful thought out loud or in your mind.

5. Keep your mind focused on your peaceful thought until the anxious one is completely gone.

directions

Circle any of the things below that might bring up anxious thoughts for you:

a test in school

meeting new people

talking with your parents

what your future holds

talking with other kids

your parents' marriage

what you look like

your report card

your family

your sexuality

class presentations

religion

performing in front of others

asking someone for a date

a particular class

your athletic skills

violence or war

money

whether or not people like you

your siblings

your body

your safety

homework

illness

Write a list of other anxious thoughts that you have had or that you struggle with frequently.

_____

_____

_____

_____

Circle any of these ideas you might use to immediately and forcefully tell yourself to STOP.

Write any other ideas you have of ways to practice telling yourself to stop.

_____

_____

Circle any of the sentences or ideas below that you might use as a peaceful thought to exchange for an anxious thought:

"I am confident."

"I am calm and relaxed."

"I am laughing with friends."

petting my cat

listening to music

running

watching floating white clouds

working out

watching a movie

vacationing

playing music

fishing

"I am lying on the beach."

"I am filled with peace."

seeing sunsets

napping

watching waves on a lake

reading

looking up on a starry night

hiking in the mountains

being with my best friend

sleeping late

camping

being with my boyfriend/girlfriend

Write a list of any other thoughts that could make you feel peaceful. Your ideas of peace may be different from someone else's, so think about what really makes you feel relaxed.

_____

_____

_____

_____

Try using the five-step thought-stopping technique over the next few days when you feel anxious. If one thought or picture doesn't work well, try different ones until you find what works the best for you.

more to do

Sometimes it is hard to identify the thought that brings on an anxious feeling. Describe any situation in which you felt anxious and couldn't identify the thought that caused your anxiety.

_____

_____

_____

_____

_____

To help discover your anxious thought, you can try the following:

- Ask yourself, "If I did know what my anxious thought was, what would it be?" Write your guess here.

_____

- Ask someone you trust to help you figure out your anxious thought. Write your guess here.

_____

Describe the thought-stopping technique in step 2 that works the best for you.

_____

_____

Write the peaceful thought that works the best for you.

_____

_____

Even if you have used the thought-stopping technique, anxious thoughts will often return. These thoughts are stubborn and may need to be stopped over and over again. When that happens, simply continue to replace your anxious thought with a peaceful one for as many times as it takes to make it stop.

_____

_____

What is the most stubborn anxious thought you have?

_____

what's the worst that could happen? 13

for you to know

When you feel anxious, you can use the question, "What is the worst that could happen?" to help lower your anxiety.

Chris couldn't decide if he should try out for the basketball team or not. He really wanted to be on the team, but thinking about tryouts raised his anxiety level so high that he didn't know if he could go through with it.

His dad told Chris to ask himself what was the very worst thing that could happen if he tried out. Chris said the worst thing would be missing every shot during the tryouts. His dad said they should think about what the odds were that the worst thing would happen. They knew Chris was a very good basketball player and he was even better at shooting than passing or dribbling. In school and shooting hoops in his driveway, he usually made 90 percent of the lay-ups he tried. If he did 10 percent worse at tryouts because he was under pressure, he would still probably make 80 percent. That was nowhere near missing every shot!

Then Chris's dad asked what would happen if, against those very high odds, Chris actually did miss every shot he tried. How would he handle it? Chris said he would feel really embarrassed. Then, he guessed, he would probably go home and have dinner, do his homework, and watch TV as usual. He would probably feel disappointed or down for a while, but eventually he would forget about it and go on with his life. He'd try out again next year.

Thinking realistically about the worst thing that could happen helped lower Chris's anxiety level. He realized that first, the odds were very slim that the worst thing would happen, and second, if it did happen, he could handle it. He then felt peaceful enough to decide he would try out for the team.

directions

In each of the spaces that follow, draw a picture or write about something that makes you feel very anxious when you think about doing it. Below that, write what you think is the worst thing that could happen if you do it. Next, circle the percentage that realistically describes the chances of this worst thing happening. Finally, describe what you would do if the worst thing did happen.

The worst thing that could happen if I do this is _____

_____

The probability of that actually happening is:

10%   20%   30%   40%   50%   60%   70%   80%   90%   100%

If it did happen, I would _____

_____

The worst thing that could happen if I do this is _____

_____

The probability of that actually happening is:

10%   20%   30%   40%   50%   60%   70%   80%   90%   100%

If it did happen, I would _____

_____

more to do

Describe how high your anxiety level was when you first considered doing each of the things you drew or wrote about.

_____

_____

_____

_____

Describe where your anxiety level is now that you have thought realistically about the worst thing that could happen.

_____

_____

_____

_____

Do you think your fears about the worst thing happening are usually realistic or not? Why?

_____

_____

_____

_____

Tell why you might or might not risk trying either one of these things now that you have thought about the worst that could happen.

_____

_____

_____

_____

If the worst thing actually did happen, what skills would help you handle each situation?

_____

14 cost-benefit analysis

Every Friday night after their football game, Andrea's school had casual dances in the field house. All of Andrea's friends went to these dances and Andrea wanted to go too, but she wouldn't. The first time she had gone to a dance she felt so anxious that she was afraid she would be sick to her stomach. She was horrified by how embarrassing that would be. Since then, Andrea was afraid to go back to another dance. Instead, she sat home on Friday nights, telling her friends that she had to babysit or she didn't feel well or she had too much homework or her parents wouldn't let her go.

Reading a book about managing anxiety, Andrea found an exercise about the costs and benefits of holding on to personal beliefs. She tried to apply it to her own situation and filled in the blanks as shown below.

Cost-Benefit Analysis

1. Write down a belief that you want to change.

    I can't go to a dance because I get so anxious I think I'll get sick.

2. Make a list of every advantage (benefit) to believing it.

    - **If I don't go, I don't have to try to dress to "look good."**

    - **I don't have to risk rejection if no one wants to dance with me.**

    - **I don't have to try to think of things to say to people I don't know well.**

3. Admit that there are good reasons to have this belief.

    I really don't like having to deal with these things. If I don't go to the dance because I believe I might get sick, then I don't have to face things that are difficult for me.

4. Make a list of every disadvantage (cost) to believing it.

    - **I feel lonely sitting at home when all my friends are at the dance.**

    - **I feel left out when everyone talks about the dance at school on Monday.**

    - **I feel bad about myself because I can't do what everyone else does.**

    - **I enjoy dancing when I'm not so anxious, and I miss it.**

    - **I miss out on the fun everyone else is having.**

    - **I hate having to make up an excuse when someone asks me why I never come to the dances.**

5. Add up both sides.

    Advantages: 3

    Disadvantages: 6

6. If there is an advantage to holding this belief, think of ways you can have that advantage without the high level of anxiety.

    I guess I could not worry so much about how I look. I could just dress nicely and then forget about it. I could also forget about someone asking me to dance. I know I can dance with my girlfriends if I want to. I could just think about enjoying my time with them and enjoying the music. I could also just plan to stay with my close friends. I don't have to talk to people I don't know well.

7. Identify the belief you would prefer to have.

    Going to a dance raises my anxiety a little, but I know once I get there I'll have fun.

activity 14 ✳ cost-benefit analysis

directions

Fill in the blanks below to do a cost-benefit analysis of a belief that raises your anxiety.

1. Write down a belief that you want to change. _____
    _____

2. Make a list of every advantage (benefit) to believing it. _____
    _____
    _____
    _____

3. Admit that there are good reasons to have this belief. _____
    _____
    _____

4. Make a list of every disadvantage (cost) to believing it. _____
    _____
    _____
    _____

5. Add up both sides. Advantages _____ Disadvantages _____

6. If there is an advantage to holding this belief, think of ways you can have the advantage without the high level of anxiety.
    _____
    _____
    _____

7. Identify the belief you would prefer to have. _____
    _____

more to do

How did you first come to have the belief that you wrote about?

_____

_____

Are you glad that you have kept this belief? Why or why not?

_____

_____

What do you think might change in your life if you stopped holding this belief?

_____

_____

How does it make you feel when you think about letting go of this belief?

_____

_____

What did you learn from filling in the cost-benefit analysis?

_____

_____

What are some steps you might have to take in order to let go of or change this belief?

_____

_____

What other beliefs do you have that you would like to change?

_____

_____

15 perfectionism

for you to know

Perfectionism is a way of thinking that often raises our anxiety level. Since complete perfection isn't actually possible for anyone to achieve, the more you try to be perfect, the more anxious you will feel because you will continually fall short of your goal.

Michael was a good student, a good baseball player, a good musician, and a good friend. A lot of kids at school liked Michael, and he got along well with his parents and his little brother, too. From the outside, it looked like Michael had much to be happy about. But Michael didn't feel happy. He felt anxious all the time. Even though Michael had nearly all As, he wasn't number one in his grade. Even though he played baseball well, he still struck out sometimes. Even though he was a good drummer and in the school band, he wasn't as good as he wanted to be. No matter how much Michael accomplished, he never stopped making mistakes, and that filled him with anxiety. When he started having headaches almost every day, his mother took him to the doctor.

The doctor couldn't find anything physically wrong with Michael, so he asked how Michael's life was going. Michael admitted that he was having a hard time. He was always anxious from pushing himself so hard but never achieving perfection. Picking up a pencil from his desk, the doctor asked Michael what he saw at its end. Michael answered, "An eraser." "Right," said the doctor, "and do you know that erasers are automatically built into pencils because it is assumed that anyone who uses a pencil will make a mistake at some time?" The doctor pointed out that pencils with erasers are sold not just to some people, but to *everyone*. No one is asked as they check out at the store, "Do you make mistakes? If so, you must buy the pencil with the eraser. If not, you can buy the pencil without the eraser."

The doctor told Michael that the pencil with an eraser is a great reminder of human imperfection. No matter how smart, strong, wise, or practiced a person is in any field at any time, they are not and cannot be perfect. They still need erasers on their pencils. He told Michael to remember the acronym PENCIL for **P**erfectionists **E**njoy **N**o **C**ontentment **I**n **L**ife.

From that day on, Michael carried a pencil with him wherever he went. He decided to change his goal from trying to be perfect to just doing the best he could. He stopped feeling anxious all the time, his headaches went away, and he started enjoying school, baseball, music, and his family a lot more.

activity 15 ✳ perfectionism

directions

Under each pair of scales below, write one thing that you try to do well in your life. On each perfection scale, draw an arrow pointing to the number that shows how hard you try to do it perfectly. On each anxiety scale draw an arrow pointing to the number that shows how anxious you feel about doing well at that activity.

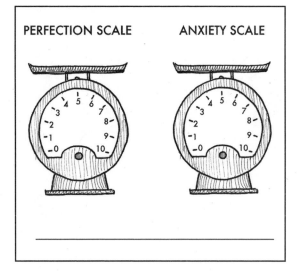

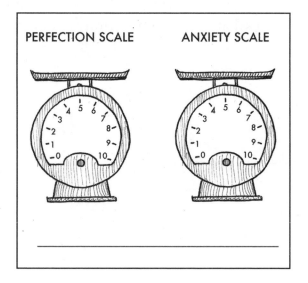

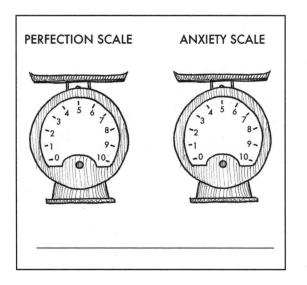

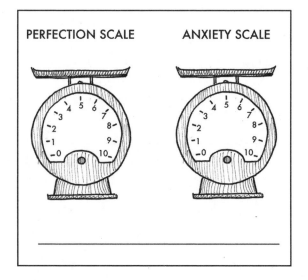

58

more to do

Look at the activities you listed. Have you ever been able to do any of them perfectly?

❏ Yes　❏ No

Do you think that if you continue to try harder and harder, you will achieve perfection in any of these things someday?

❏ Yes　❏ No

Look at your rating scales. Notice which activities make you more anxious: those that you try to do perfectly or those where you allow yourself to be imperfect.

How would your anxiety level change if you didn't try to do these activities perfectly?

_____

_____

People often think that they are doing a better job if they try to do things perfectly. Actually, the opposite is true. Perfectionists tend to achieve less in the long run because of their inability to complete tasks and make final decisions. In the excessive amount of time the perfectionist spends correcting and refining the "unacceptable," the nonperfectionist can accomplish twice as much work that is acceptable.

Can you think of a time when trying to do something perfectly actually caused you to do a worse job? If so, describe it here.

_____

_____

_____

_____

_____

16 letting go of control

for you to know

It is normal for people to want to have control over what happens in their life. But in reality, there are many, many things we cannot control, no matter how hard we try. Because it is an impossible task, trying to have control over everything and everyone can raise your anxiety level. When you are able to let go of the need to control everything, your anxiety level will be lower.

Matt felt best when everything went the way he planned it. He liked his life to be in order, and he liked to be in charge of it. That worked fine as long as he was able to stay in control, but when unexpected things happened, or when people didn't act the way he wanted them to, Matt would get very anxious.

One week, Matt had a harder time than usual. His best friend decided to go to a ball game with another friend instead of watching videos with Matt. His English teacher wouldn't give him an extra day to finish his paper. On his paper route, he made ten dollars less in tips than he had hoped for. As these things that he couldn't control happened, Matt felt like his whole life was falling apart.

Matt's mom noticed that he seemed very anxious when she drove him to school. He told her what had been happening and how frustrated he was. He couldn't make things be the way he wanted them to be. Matt's mom told him that no one can control everything and that was okay. He would survive. He needed to let go of trying to control those things and put his focus back on the things he could control.

Matt tried to take her advice. When he started feeling anxious about his friend, his English teacher, and his tips, he tried to remind himself that these things were out of his control but that he was okay. He found another friend to hang out with Friday night, handed in the best paper he could, and just accepted that he hadn't made as much money as he'd planned. When he was able to let go, he felt much more peaceful.

directions

Circle the response that tells how much control you have over each of these situations:

If I will have fun at a party	No control	Some control	Complete control
If everyone in school will like me	No control	Some control	Complete control
If I will break the swim team record	No control	Some control	Complete control
If I study hard for a test	No control	Some control	Complete control
If my parents will get divorced	No control	Some control	Complete control
If the person I like will ask me to dance	No control	Some control	Complete control
If I eat too much	No control	Some control	Complete control
If my friend will agree to see the movie I want to see	No control	Some control	Complete control
If it will rain on the day of my pool party	No control	Some control	Complete control
If my science project partner will work as hard as I do	No control	Some control	Complete control
If the teacher will give me a break on my grade	No control	Some control	Complete control
If I will get an award	No control	Some control	Complete control
If my best friends will spend as much time with me as I want them to	No control	Some control	Complete control
If my friend will take my advice	No control	Some control	Complete control
If my parents will give me the privileges I want	No control	Some control	Complete control
If I am a kind person	No control	Some control	Complete control

more to do

Make a list of the things, situations, or people you try to control. Next to each item you have listed, write "no," "some," or "complete" to tell how much control you have over it.

_____   _____

_____   _____

_____   _____

_____   _____

_____   _____

Which of these would be the hardest to let go of trying to control, and why? _____

_____

_____

What does trying to let go of control feel like? _____

_____

_____

What do you think will happen if you let go of control? _____

_____

_____

The thought of letting go can make some people feel more anxious at first. But once they become comfortable and know that they will be safe even if they do not control everything, they change their expectations and are able to lower their anxiety level.

If you have trouble letting go of control, try doing or redoing Activity 12: Thought Stopping, Activity 13: What's the Worst That Could Happen, or Activity 32: A Higher Power.

positive affirmations 17

for you to know

People send mental messages to themselves all throughout the day. These messages are called "affirmations" because they affirm and reinforce ideas. Sending yourself negative affirmations will increase your anxiety level. Sending yourself positive affirmations will help you to feel more peaceful.

Joshua's daily anxiety level was pretty high, even when nothing especially stressful was going on. He didn't understand how his friends could be so carefree when there were so many things he felt anxious about. His counselor suggested that Joshua work on changing his affirmations. Instead of telling himself things that raised his anxiety, he could tell himself things that helped him feel more peaceful. First, Joshua had to identify his current affirmations. Here are some of the messages he noticed that were constantly running through his head:

- "I've got so much homework; I'll never get it all done."

- "Everyone is so much more confident than me; I'm so insecure."

- "I don't have good enough grades; I'll never get into a good college."

- "Those kids are laughing; they must be laughing at the way I look."

Joshua didn't realize how often he played these affirmations in his head until he started paying attention to them. He also noticed that whenever he heard one of them, he felt a pang of anxiety. He talked with his counselor about his wish to change his affirmations from negative to positive. Together, they decided on the following changes:

- "I can get my homework done because I use my time wisely."

- "I have a lot to be confident about! I'm a kind person, a good friend, and a great soccer player."

- "My grades are definitely good enough to get me into college; I know there will be a good match for me.

- "People laugh about a million different things. It doesn't have to be about me."

Joshua practiced these new, positive affirmations and found himself feeling happier and less anxious. He continued to monitor his self-messages on a regular basis and made a conscious effort to change them from negative to positive.

directions

Pay attention to your own affirmations for the next two days. Using the chart below, record the messages you hear, how many times you hear them in one day, and whether they are negative or positive. Then rewrite any negative messages, changing them to positive.

My Affirmation	Times Heard	Negative or Positive	New Message

more to do

Look at your first list of affirmations. Tell how long you have been sending yourself these messages and where you think you first got these ideas.

_____

_____

_____

Describe how these messages affect your anxiety level.

_____

_____

_____

Describe how each of the rewritten positive messages affects your anxiety level.

_____

_____

_____

Changing affirmations doesn't happen overnight. Many of them may have been with you since you were very young and will take a while to change. Sometimes people feel a little anxious about changing their affirmations. Describe any concerns you have and tell why.

_____

_____

_____

If you never changed your negative affirmations, how do you think they would continue to affect your anxiety level?

_____

_____

_____

18 serenity, courage, and wisdom

for you to know

You can reduce feelings of anxiety by using serenity, courage, and wisdom. That means you step back and evaluate the situation you are in, determine the difference between the things you can and cannot change, and then act on your knowledge.

Gabriella was talking with her aunt about some problems with her friends. Two of her best friends had gotten into an argument and weren't talking to each other. Gabriella wasn't fighting with either of them, but she felt as if she was in the middle of their argument. Each friend would talk to her negatively about the other, and that made Gabriella uncomfortable. She wished they would make up and get over it, but they were both so stubborn that neither one would apologize first. When Gabriella was with either of them, she felt very anxious. She didn't want to lose her best friends, but she wasn't enjoying being with them much anymore.

Gabriella's aunt told her about a tool she used to help herself let go of anxiety. She told Gabriella to say to herself, "I have the serenity to accept the things I cannot change, the courage to change the things I can, and the wisdom to know the difference."

Gabriella repeated the words, and then her aunt helped her step back and look at the situation carefully. They talked about the fact that Gabriella couldn't force her friends to apologize—that was something she had to accept that she couldn't change. However, she could tell them that she didn't want to be placed in the middle anymore. And she could decide to walk away or not to listen when they complained about each other—that was something she could change.

Gabriella repeated the words once more, "I have the serenity to accept the things I cannot change, the courage to change the things I can, and the wisdom to know the difference." She soon felt more peaceful as she thought about using serenity, courage, and wisdom to help herself.

directions

The kids in the pictures below are feeling anxious about their situations. Next to each picture, write what they can change and what they cannot change about what is going on. At the bottom of the page, write Gabriella's words about serenity, courage, and wisdom.

_____

_____

_____

_____

_____

_____

_____

_____

_____

_____

_____

_____

_____

_____

_____

_____

more to do

Describe a situation that you have been feeling anxious about in your own life lately.

_____

_____

_____

_____

Think about the situation carefully and realistically. List the things that you can actually change about this situation.

_____

_____

_____

_____

List the things that you really cannot change.

_____

_____

_____

_____

How will it affect your life if you accept the things you cannot change?

_____

_____

_____

_____

Are you able to feel serene about it? Tell why or why not.

_____

_____

_____

_____

Do you have the courage to change the things you can change? Tell why or why not.

_____

_____

_____

_____

What might help you feel more courageous?

_____

_____

_____

_____

Write Gabriella's words about serenity, courage, and wisdom here. Read the words out loud and then sign your name below them.

_____

_____

_____

Make a copy of this quote with your signature, cut it out, and put it in your wallet or notebook so you can carry it with you. If you start feeling anxious, take it out and read it over.

19 seeing the bigger picture

for you to know

Sometimes people focus so closely on one or two small details of a situation that they lose sight of the bigger picture—the whole context—that those details are in. Focusing too closely on an anxious thought makes your anxiety level rise higher. Shifting your focus to the bigger picture can help you to feel more peaceful.

Ryan was feeling anxious because his history teacher had asked him to be the first one to give his oral report the next day. Ryan's older brother, Joe, could tell that something was bothering Ryan and asked what it was. When Ryan told him, Joe said Ryan should look at the bigger picture: Ryan already had a solid B in the class and one presentation wasn't going to change that. The teacher liked him and knew he was a hard worker. He was well prepared for his report and had excellent visual aids. If he did his report first, he would get it over with and could relax for the rest of the week while the other kids did theirs. When Ryan reconsidered his one detail of anxiety in light of this bigger picture, he felt much more peaceful.

directions

Focusing on one detail of Ryan's situation was like looking at it through binoculars. It made the detail—and his anxiety—appear bigger, like the picture on the left. When he focused on the situation as a whole, it was like looking at that detail through the other end of the binoculars, like the picture on the right.

activity 19 ✳ seeing the bigger picture

In the box on the left, draw or write about a detail of your own life that raises your anxiety level, as if you were looking at it through binoculars. In the box on the right, draw or write that same detail as if you were looking through the other end of the binoculars so that you are able to see the detail in the context of the bigger picture. Then add the other details of the bigger picture around the detail that makes you anxious.

more to do

Look at your two pictures. Describe the difference in your anxious detail when you look at it alone and when you see it in the bigger picture.

_____

_____

_____

For each sentence below, tell if your anxiety would be low, medium, or high, first focusing only on the detail, then focusing on the bigger picture.

Detail: You failed a math test.	low	medium	high
Bigger picture: You got Bs on all of your other math tests for the entire year.	low	medium	high
Detail: You struck out when playing a game of baseball.	low	medium	high
Bigger picture: Your last three at-bats before that were base hits.	low	medium	high
Detail: You hit a wrong note during your trombone solo.	low	medium	high
Bigger picture: You got enthusiastic applause.	low	medium	high
Detail: Someone in your class called you a nerd.	low	medium	high
Bigger picture: You have five good friends who would do anything for you.	low	medium	high
Detail: The first time you went to a dance, your date was bored and went home early with someone else.	low	medium	high
Bigger picture: After your date left, three different people asked you to dance.	low	medium	high

How is your anxiety level affected by shifting your focus from one anxious detail to the bigger picture?

_____

_____

_____

20 talking it out

for you to know

When people hold feelings of anxiety inside and do not express them, the anxiety does not just disappear. In fact, holding anxiety in can actually make it feel more overwhelming. Expressing anxiety by talking about it helps to release it.

Kelly felt a lot of anxiety whenever she was going to perform in a school play. She was a good actress with a beautiful singing voice, and she often got the lead role in the play. But even though people told her she was very talented, she still felt anxious every time she had to go on stage.

Kelly didn't like talking about her feelings. She was afraid that if she talked about the anxiety, she would feel it even more. She was also concerned that the other kids might think she was weird or wimpy if she told them how anxious she felt. So instead of saying anything, she just tried to ignore it.

By the end of the school year, Kelly had started to get bad stomachaches whenever she had to go on stage. Her mother took her to the doctor for a checkup, but he couldn't find anything physically wrong. Kelly had known her doctor since she was very young, and she felt comfortable telling him about her anxiety. She explained that her stomachaches came only before she performed.

The doctor said Kelly's stomachaches were a result of holding her anxiety inside. He said she needed to start letting it out, or the stomachaches would get worse. He suggested that she talk with her drama teacher about how she felt. When Kelly did, she learned that the other kids also felt anxious before a performance. The drama teacher started encouraging all his students to share their feelings of anxiety. Even just saying, "Wow, I'm a little nervous. Are you?" helped to release it. As Kelly learned to talk about her feelings, her stomachaches came less often and finally went away altogether.

directions

Each of the pictures below shows something that is being filled. Describe what will happen in each case if the item is filled beyond its capacity.

more to do

Look at the pictures of the items being filled. What are some things that might happen when a person becomes too full of anxiety?

_____

_____

_____

What are some things that happen to you when you do not let out your anxious feelings?

_____

_____

_____

Why do you think Kelly was able to share her feelings of anxiety with her doctor when she hadn't wanted to share them with anyone else?

_____

_____

_____

What do you think made Kelly change her mind about sharing her anxious feelings with her classmates?

_____

_____

_____

How do you feel about talking about your anxiety with other people?

_____

_____

_____

Circle any of the following people with whom you might feel comfortable talking about your anxiety:

best friend	father	aunt or uncle
doctor	cousin	coach
school counselor	grandparent	friend
mother	employer	sibling
professional counselor	teacher	worship leader

Write the names of anyone else in your life with whom you might feel comfortable talking about your anxiety.

_____

_____

_____

Circle any of the phrases below that you might say to express anxious feelings:

I am so nervous!

I'm a little anxious about this.

I can feel my heart pounding; I must be nervous.

I am really anxious about doing this.

I'm feeling a lot of anxiety right now.

I'm really stressing about this.

Write any other words that you could use to express your feelings of anxiety.

_____

_____

21 writing it out

for you to know

Writing can be an effective way to express and release feelings of anxiety. You don't need any special kind of writing talent because you are writing for yourself only.

Sean's counselor suggested that he start keeping a journal so he would have a private place to express his feelings of anxiety. Sean didn't know if he liked that idea. English had never been his best subject, and he hated having to write outlines and remember correct grammar and punctuation. His counselor said that Sean didn't have to worry about any of those things in his journal. Journal writing is personal. No one else has to be able to read it, so the writing doesn't have to be clear or organized or correctly punctuated. He said the journal was one place where Sean could write without using any of the rules he had learned in English class.

Sean decided to give it a try. The next time he felt anxious was right before gym class. They were starting a unit on volleyball, and Sean thought he was the worst volleyball player in the world. He thought his serve and his aim were poor, and he always felt like such an idiot when he missed the ball. He could feel his jaw muscles getting tight just thinking about it. Before going to gym, he took out his journal and started to write down what he was feeling. He didn't pay attention to how his writing looked; he just focused on getting his anxiety out. He found himself writing pretty fast at first, but as the emotion lost some of its power, he started slowing down. After a couple of paragraphs, Sean realized that he felt more peaceful. He still wasn't excited about volleyball, but he thought he could handle it. He was surprised when he actually missed fewer shots than usual on the court that day. His counselor said that was probably because he wasn't feeling as anxious, so he had better focus and control over his body.

directions

In the first space below, write all the English composition rules you can think of. In the second space, try writing a paragraph or two about your anxious feelings *without* using any of those rules.

Composition Rules

_____

_____

_____

_____

_____

_____

Writing Without Rules

_____

_____

_____

_____

_____

_____

_____

more to do

People are so used to following English rules when they write that sometimes it is hard to try to write without them. Describe what it was like for you.

_____

_____

_____

Try writing about your feelings the next time you feel anxious. Or at one time during the day, take the time to write about your anxious feelings in the past twenty-four hours. Tell how it felt to express these feelings on paper.

_____

_____

When you write to release anxiety, you can use any kind of writing materials you like. The only important thing is that you are comfortable. Some people like to write in spiral notebooks with blue ink, some like to write on unlined paper with pencils or felt-tipped markers, and some like to write at the computer. What writing materials are you most comfortable with?

_____

Sometimes people are afraid that if they write about their anxious feelings, someone else will find and read what they have written. If that is true for you, you will need to find a way to maintain your privacy. Here are some options:

Shred your writing after you're done.

Keep your writing in a locked drawer.

Write so messily that no one can read it.

Keep your writing where no one will find it.

Throw your writing away when you're done.

Write in a book with a lock on it.

Write in code.

Circle any of the above ideas that might work for you. Write any other ideas you have here.

_____

_____

83

22 eating and anxiety

for you to know

What you eat and drink can have an effect on your anxiety level. Some foods and beverages have a chemical makeup that can cause you to feel more anxious. Some foods and beverages have a chemical makeup that can help you to lower your anxiety.

Everyone's body is a little different from everyone else's. We each have a unique chemical makeup that reacts with the chemicals in everything we ingest. A number of substances have been linked to increased anxiety in many people. Some of these are caffeine, refined white sugar, refined white flour, alcohol, and some artificial sweeteners. A number of other substances have been linked to keeping anxiety low. Some of these are B-complex vitamins (such as niacin, thiamin, riboflavin, B-6, B-12, biotin, pantothenic acid, and folic acid), calcium, magnesium, omega-3 fatty acids, and complex carbohydrates.

You may be aware of ingesting some of these substances. When you sprinkle sugar on your cereal, you know you are eating sugar. Other substances have unfamiliar names and are not so obvious. Most people do not know when they are ingesting folic acid. To be fully aware of everything you are putting into your body, you may have to read the labels on the packages of the foods you eat. To learn more about their chemical makeup, you can also look up individual foods in an encyclopedia or a book on nutrition, or on the Internet.

Some of the more common foods that contain these substances are listed below.

Substances that may raise your anxiety level and foods they are found in:

Caffeine: coffee, tea, chocolate, soda

Refined white sugar: nondiet soda, candy, cookies, cakes, ice cream, other desserts, sugar-coated cereals

Refined white flour: white bread and rolls, hamburger buns, spaghetti and other white pasta, pretzels

Alcohol: beer, wine, hard liquor

Artificial sweeteners: diet soda, most foods labeled "diet," many sugar-free products, cereals

Substances that may lower your anxiety level and foods they are found in:

Niacin: chicken, turkey, wheat, brown rice, tuna

Thiamin: oats, wheat, pork, tuna, asparagus, sunflower seeds, white rice

Riboflavin: milk, yogurt, pork, avocados, mushrooms

Vitamin B-6: turkey, bananas, mangoes, sunflower seeds, sweet potatoes, tuna, pork

Vitamin B-12: beef, yogurt, tuna, crab, clams

Biotin: eggs, cheese, peanuts, cauliflower

Pantothenic acid: yogurt, avocados, salmon, sunflower seeds, mushrooms

Folic acid: turkey, oranges, peas, avocados, cabbage, broccoli, soybeans

Calcium: milk, yogurt, cheese, broccoli, spinach

Magnesium: spinach, almonds, avocados, sunflower seeds, Brazil nuts

Omega-3 fatty acids: tuna, salmon, sardines, walnuts, dark green leafy vegetables, soybeans

Complex carbohydrates: whole-grain breads, whole-grain cereals, whole-grain pasta, brown rice

directions

Make seven copies of the diary below. For the next week, record your anxiety level four times a day, and write down everything that you eat and drink. Measure your anxiety by rating it with a number from 0 to 10 (0 being completely peaceful and 10 being highly anxious).

Day _____	
My Anxiety Level	**What I Ate**
Waking up	
Midday	
6:00 PM	
Bedtime	

more to do

Looking back at your diary, describe the difference between the number of anxiety-raising substances you ingested and the number of anxiety-lowering substances you ingested.

_____

_____

Look at the times when you rated yourself as highly anxious. Then look at your food intake for the twenty-four hours preceding that. Describe any connection you notice between high anxiety and what you ate or drank.

_____

_____

Look at the times when you rated your anxiety as very low. Then look at your food intake for the twenty-four hours preceding that. Describe any connection you notice between low anxiety and what you ate or drank.

_____

_____

Do you see any patterns in your anxiety level and food or beverage intake? ❑ Yes ❑ No

Sometimes people's favorite foods are those that raise anxiety. It can be hard to give those up completely, but even cutting back on anxiety-raising substances can be helpful. Think about some specific, realistic ways you can ingest fewer substances that raise your anxiety level, and describe those ways here.

_____

_____

Think about some specific, realistic ways you can ingest more substances that lower your anxiety level, and describe those ways here.

_____

_____

This activity provided you with only a partial list of foods that may raise or lower anxiety. You can get a more complete list from a dietitian or a nutritionist or from reading materials they suggest.

more exercise, less anxiety 23

for you to know

Participating in almost any kind of physical exercise can help lower your anxiety level. Exercising on a regular basis can prevent anxiety. Exercising at the time you feel anxious can release tension right at that moment.

Megan was having a hard time getting along with her family. It felt like her parents were constantly nagging her and her brother and sister were constantly bothering her. It made her so anxious that sometimes she felt she would explode. One afternoon at home, everyone seemed to be irritating her at once. She knew she had to get away from them before she said or did something impulsive that would get her into trouble. Megan walked out the front door of her house and started jogging down the street. By the time she got around the block, she noticed that she felt better. Her anxiety had decreased. She was breathing more deeply, and her mind was clearing. Megan continued to jog for ten more minutes until she felt completely calm. As she walked the last block home, she realized that she felt more peaceful than she had in a long time. Her whole body was relaxed, she felt healthy and strong, and her irritation had subsided. She went back into the house and was then able to talk calmly with her family. She even shared with them how much better she felt after her run.

Megan's mom was a physical education teacher. She explained to Megan that when we feel anxious, our glands send a hormone called adrenaline into our bodies. Adrenaline is what makes our muscles tense and our heart beat faster. When we exercise, the adrenaline is expelled, our muscles relax, and our heart rate slows down again. She explained to Megan that regular exercise was one of the best ways to keep daily anxiety at a lower, manageable level.

Megan started running three times a week, whether she was feeling anxious at the time or not. She noticed that she always felt great for a few hours after her run and that it was then easier for her to feel peaceful for the rest of the day.

activity 23 ✱ more exercise, less anxiety

directions

A wide variety of physical activities are listed below. Put a star next to any activity that you know you really enjoy. Put a "T" next to any activity you have never done but would really like to try.

baseball	basketball	skiing	swimming
hiking	tennis	biking	snow boarding
football	karate	running	bowling
gymnastics	wrestling	archery	golf
paintball	laser tag	dance	race walking
volleyball	badminton	judo	waterskiing
tubing	lacrosse	soccer	bocce ball
lifting weights	aerobic dance	kickboxing	racquetball
diving	rappelling	surfing	wind surfing

Looking at the activities you starred, write down those that would be easiest for you to do on a regular basis. What time of day and where would be most realistic for you to do these?

_____

_____

Write down one or two times and days over the next week when you can exercise. Write them in your schedule book or on your calendar, and then follow through on your plan.

_____

_____

Notice your anxiety level both before and after you exercise. Describe what you notice.

_____

_____

_____

more to do

Which exercises from the list might you be able to do right at the moment you are feeling anxious?

_____

_____

Describe a recent situation that made you anxious and tell how you could have performed some exercise at that time to relieve your anxiety.

_____

_____

_____

_____

From the list of activities you put a "T" next to, choose one or two you could try in the next couple of weeks. Write your plan here for how you can realistically make it happen.

_____

_____

_____

_____

activity 23 * more exercise, less anxiety

After you try these new activities, write about your experience and whether or not you would like to do these activities again.

_____

_____

_____

_____

_____

_____

_____

_____

_____

_____

_____

_____

peaceful movement 24

for you to know

Certain types of physical movement can help people relieve anxiety and feel more peaceful. When you practice these movements on a regular basis, you can keep anxiety at a lower level.

Here are three common types of peaceful movement.

1. Relaxed Stretching

Stretching is simply the gentle, sustained movement of elongating your muscles. When you stretch your muscles, you help to dissipate the stress chemicals that have collected in them and you increase the blood circulation in your body, both of which help relieve anxiety. If you breathe peacefully and deeply while you stretch, you help bring oxygen to all of your muscle groups, also relieving anxiety.

Stretching is one of the easiest anxiety-reducing techniques you can use because you can stretch almost any muscle group at any time, almost anywhere you are. You don't need special equipment or a large block of time. You don't need any particular athletic skill or ability.

It is important to stretch slowly and gently so that you don't overextend your muscles. If you stretch a little every day on a regular basis, you will help keep your anxiety level low. If you take a stretching break when you are feeling particularly tense about something, it will help you release and manage feelings of anxiety. Stretching all of your muscles will help keep them relaxed and flexible. Stretching the particular muscles where you hold most of your tension will help to bring relief in that particular area.

2. Yoga

Yoga is a science of life that originated in India thousands of years ago. Its philosophy strives to unify body, mind, and spirit through exercise, breathing, and meditation in order to maintain balance and health in life.

The physical exercises, or postures, learned in yoga are designed to increase the health of the glandular system in your body. The stretching involved tones your muscles and joints as well as your entire skeletal system. Breathing exercises help to increase and maintain your health through breath control, bringing energy to your body and developing peacefulness. Meditation develops a quiet mind and releases anxiety as well as increasing your mental power and concentration.

The goal of yoga is to develop a state of inner peace. Practice does not involve any special equipment or clothing, but some beginning instruction is necessary to learn the postures and the correct positioning of your body.

3. T'ai Chi

T'ai Chi is a practice of movement stemming from Chinese culture. While historically it was considered a martial art and a form of nonviolent self-defense, it is widely practiced in Western cultures today as a form of "moving meditation." Movements in T'ai Chi are performed softly and gracefully with smooth, even transitions between them.

Along with stimulating the flow of "chi," or energy, throughout the body and increasing health and vitality, T'ai Chi movements foster a calm and tranquil mind, help you to relax and relieve tension, and reverse the effects of stress on your body and mind. The slow, meditative movements of T'ai Chi make it a helpful practice for relaxation, balance, and physical and emotional health.

As with yoga, T'ai Chi requires instruction to help you begin, but once you have learned a number of movements, you can continue to practice alone, for either prevention or management of anxiety.

Even just a few minutes of peaceful movement when you wake up in the morning can set a peaceful tone for your whole day. The same activity at midday can help you recenter yourself and come back to a place of balance. Done right before you go to sleep at night, peaceful movement can help you sleep more deeply and restfully.

directions

You can learn how to do relaxed stretching, yoga, and T'ai Chi by taking classes through your school, park district, fitness center, or other educational facility. You can also try out any of these activities first by asking if you can visit a class or by watching tapes or DVDs that you can buy, rent from a video store, or borrow from your library. Trying out these activities first can give you an idea of which one you feel most comfortable with and which one suits you the best.

Find a way to try each of these types of movement at least once. Each time you try a new technique, pay attention to your anxiety level before and after your practice. Rate your anxiety level by giving it a number on a scale from 0 to 10 (0 being completely peaceful and 10 being highly anxious). Record your ratings here.

Relaxed Stretching

Anxiety level before one session of relaxed stretching:

| 0 | 1 | 2 | 3 | 4 | 5 | 6 | 7 | 8 | 9 | 10 |

Anxiety level after one session of relaxed stretching:

| 0 | 1 | 2 | 3 | 4 | 5 | 6 | 7 | 8 | 9 | 10 |

Yoga

Anxiety level before one session of yoga:

| 0 | 1 | 2 | 3 | 4 | 5 | 6 | 7 | 8 | 9 | 10 |

Anxiety level after one session of yoga:

| 0 | 1 | 2 | 3 | 4 | 5 | 6 | 7 | 8 | 9 | 10 |

T'ai Chi

Anxiety level before one session of T'ai Chi:

| 0 | 1 | 2 | 3 | 4 | 5 | 6 | 7 | 8 | 9 | 10 |

Anxiety level after one session of T'ai Chi:

| 0 | 1 | 2 | 3 | 4 | 5 | 6 | 7 | 8 | 9 | 10 |

more to do

Tell which of the movement activities you liked best, and why.

_____

_____

Tell which of the movement activities you liked least, and why.

_____

_____

Rate the three movement activities in the order of their effectiveness for lowering your anxiety level, with 1 being the most and 3 being the least effective.

_____ Relaxed Stretching   _____ Yoga   _____ T'ai Chi

Tell how easy or difficult it was for you to do a slow-moving activity, and why.

_____

_____

Sometimes people actually get a little more anxious when they first try a peaceful movement activity. They may be nervous about doing it "right" or they may not be used to having their bodies moving so quietly or slowly. If that happened to you, describe your experience.

_____

_____

_____

If any of these movement activities were enjoyable or helpful in lowering your anxiety level, try to practice them for five minutes a day or more, on a regular basis. That will help you release anxiety and stay more peaceful throughout the whole day. Write down a time of day that you could spend five minutes practicing peaceful movement.

_____

It can take some people a number of tries before they become comfortable with a peaceful movement activity. Try not to give up until you have really given it a chance.

25 progressive relaxation

You can use progressive relaxation for anxiety prevention by practicing it on a regular basis. That will help keep your daily anxiety level lower. You can also use progressive relaxation as intervention on a day when your anxiety level is higher than usual.

Ideally, you will have a quiet place and fifteen or twenty minutes each time you practice progressive relaxation. If you have a busy schedule and find it hard to make that happen, you can do a brief variation of this exercise, just about any place at any time. When you are sitting in class, in the bleachers, in the passenger seat of the car, in a restaurant, or in the library, you can take a few minutes to focus on consciously relaxing your muscles. Any effort you make can help you release and relieve anxiety.

directions

Read this exercise all the way through carefully before you try it. If possible, find a quiet place without distractions to practice. You might want to have someone help you with this exercise the first few times you try it. Simply ask the person to slowly read the directions as you sit with your eyes closed, following them.

Progressive Relaxation

Sit in a comfortable position and loosen any tight clothing so that you don't feel cramped or constrained and can breathe easily. You may lie down if you wish, as long as you know you won't fall asleep. Before you start, rate your anxiety level on a scale from 0 to 10 (0 being completely peaceful and 10 being highly anxious). Write your number down, tell it to another person, or remember it so you can use it later.

Close your eyes and for a few minutes put your attention on your breath. You don't have to try to change your breathing at all—simply notice it. Instead of trying to direct your breath, just follow it. All you have to do is notice where it is at any moment and where it goes at the next moment. As you inhale and exhale, your breath may move in and out of your mouth or nostrils; it may move into your throat, neck, or lungs or even down into your diaphragm. Your breath may make your shoulders rise and fall or your chest move up and down. It may cause a tickle or a light sensation in your body at any point. There is no right or wrong way to experience your breath; just notice where it goes and continue to follow it.

When your breath becomes rhythmic and even, move your attention to the top of your head. Notice if you are holding any tension around your facial area or the muscles surrounding your skull. Imagine all of this tension leaving your head and being pulled out into the air around you. After it leaves your head, it simply floats away off into space. You notice that your forehead, your cheeks, your chin, and your jaw are all completely free of tension and relaxed. Your face and jaw are so relaxed that your mouth may drop open a little.

Now move your attention to your neck. Picture any tension that you may be holding in the back or front of your neck as leaving your body and floating off into space. Consciously release the muscles in your neck and let go of any tension in this area.

Next, pay attention to your shoulders and upper back. Notice if you are holding any tension here. Many people hold anxiety in these areas. Consciously release any tension you are holding here. Feel the release and relief as you let the tension go. Feel your shoulders drop a little as the tension leaves your body.

Move your attention now to your chest and lungs. Know that you are releasing any and all tension from this area of your body. Your lungs are contracting and expanding freely. Your chest is rising and falling peacefully and rhythmically as you breathe. Any tension that was in your chest or lungs has now left. Your muscles here are completely relaxed.

Next, focus on your upper arms. Picture the muscles in your arms relaxing. These muscles work hard each day, helping you lift and carry. Right now they don't have to do anything, so let them relax. Release any tension that you might be holding in your upper arms and then in your lower arms and your hands and fingers. Concentrate on releasing any tightness you may be carrying anywhere along your arms. Picture the tension simply flowing down your arms and out the ends of your fingertips. Your arms are now completely relaxed.

Move your focus to your stomach. It is common for people to feel tightness or "knots" in their stomach when they are anxious. Pay attention to your stomach muscles and consciously relax them. Each time you exhale, let them become more and more limp, until you feel your stomach "sinking" comfortably into your body. Know that any tension in your stomach is now gone, and your stomach is completely relaxed.

Now place your attention on your lower back and hips. Release any tension you may be feeling in these areas. Let your hips feel warm and heavy, and feel them sinking comfortably into the chair beneath you. Let the muscles in your lower back and hips relax completely and notice how good this feels.

Next, move your attention to your upper legs. There are large muscles in your thighs that carry you from place to place every day. They don't need to do any work right now, so you can let them relax completely. Let your upper legs feel warm and heavy. Let them sink into the chair beneath you as you release all the tension from this area of your body. Notice how relaxed your thighs are now.

Move down your legs to your knees and calves, your feet and toes. These body parts also work hard to hold you up every day. They can be completely relaxed now. Consciously let any tension go from these muscle groups and joints. Picture the tension flowing easily out of your legs and your feet and out the tips of your toes. Let all of this tension disappear into the air around you.

Now sit quietly for a few minutes and enjoy the relaxation you have allowed in your body. Notice what it's like to be this relaxed. Rate your anxiety level once again, as you did before you started this exercise. Notice if your number has gone up, down, or stayed the same. When you are ready, bring your attention back to the room you are in, and open your eyes.

more to do

The goal of this activity is to reduce anxiety. Sometimes it will initially raise people's anxiety because they aren't used to sitting quietly or with their eyes closed. With practice, it will get more comfortable.

Describe what it was like for you to do this activity.

_____

_____

_____

Tell what your anxiety ratings were before and after the exercise. Tell why you think your anxiety level went up, down, or stayed the same.

_____

_____

_____

List any places in your body that you noticed tension. Circle those where you have noticed tension at previous times when you have been anxious. Know that you can pay attention to those places and make an effort to consciously relax them when they become tense.

_____

_____

_____

Tell what it was like to have your body completely relaxed.

_____

_____

_____

centering yourself 26

for you to know

When you focus your attention and energy on the physical center of your body, you can help yourself manage anxiety by gaining balance and stability.

Annie had a hard time managing anxiety when she had to do a lot of things in a short period of time. One evening when she was babysitting for her neighbor, she found herself holding the baby on her hip while she stood at the stove cooking macaroni and cheese for the six-year-old, who was crying because she had just spilled her soda. At the same time, the phone rang, and Annie noticed that the dog was chewing through the straps of her backpack. Annie felt scattered and frazzled and like she wanted to scream. Then she remembered the centering exercise she had learned in health class.

Instead of screaming, Annie took just a few seconds and focused on the center of gravity in her body. She pictured herself pulling all her scattered energy into her central point of strength and balance. By focusing on this center for a short time, she was able to regain her composure and act from that core of peace rather than from an anxious state. She turned off the stove burner, set the baby in the high chair, moved the backpack from the floor to the table, grabbed a roll of paper towels to soak up the soda, and let the answering machine get the phone.

Annie found that she could use centering to help herself feel grounded and balanced whenever she started to feel anxious. She used the exercise before her ice-skating competition, as her history teacher was passing out the final exam, when her little brother was irritating her, and as she approached the guy she had a crush on. Practicing centering helped Annie remain peaceful.

directions

To find your center, or the geographic middle of your physical body, look at the picture below and then try this activity. You may want to have someone read it to you as you stand with your eyes closed.

Stand straight with both feet flat and solidly on the floor, shoulder-width apart. Close your eyes. Adjust yourself so that you feel balanced. Place your attention on your physical body. Without moving or touching your right hand, put your attention on it. Now without moving or touching your left knee, put your attention on it. Next, without moving or touching your navel, put your attention on it. Now be aware of a spot an inch or two behind and two or three inches below your navel, in the back center of your abdomen. With your eyes closed, try to get a sense of this inner spot that is the center of gravity of your body.

Keep your attention focused on this point. Imagine yourself drawing in all your scattered energy and concentrating it here. Continue to focus your energy here for a few minutes until you feel stable and balanced.

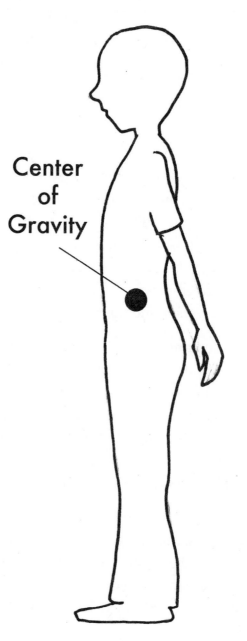

Center of Gravity

more to do

Sometimes people find it hard to locate their center of gravity on the first try. If you had trouble finding it, try the activity again when you are feeling calm. Tell what it was like when you tried again.

_____

_____

Describe any common situations in your life in which you feel that your energy gets scattered and you feel anxious.

_____

_____

_____

Describe a situation you encountered in the past week in which you felt anxious. At what point could you have taken a few seconds to center yourself so that you could act from a point of balance rather than anxiety?

_____

_____

_____

Once you have a good sense of where your center is, you don't have to be standing up to practice. You can center yourself while you are alone in your bedroom, sitting in class, or walking through the mall. Try to practice regaining your balance in different situations as you go through your week.

Describe a situation in which centering helped you let go of anxiety and feel more stable.

_____

_____

_____

27 mindfulness

for you to know

Mindfulness is the act of keeping your focus on the present moment. When you practice mindfulness on a regular basis, it can help to keep your anxiety at a lower level. Practicing mindfulness at the time you feel high anxiety can help you to manage it and bring yourself back to a peaceful state.

Being mindful means that you are paying attention to, and therefore living in, the present moment. Most of the time, our minds are reaching forward to the future, and we often start to worry about things that are unknown. That raises our anxiety level. Or our minds are reaching back into the past, and we may feel guilt or regret about something we have done or said. That raises our anxiety level, too.

Being mindful means being accepting and nonjudgmental about whatever is happening in the present moment. It is often our nature to be critical of ourselves, others, and our environment. This kind of judging rarely changes anyone or anything, but it does raise our anxiety level.

Focusing on the present moment can help you let go of anxiety. For example, if you are playing basketball, just focus on playing basketball. Watch your hands and the ball soaring through the air and feel the sweat on your forehead. You can't worry about your final exams or your recital or your job if you are just thinking about the ball. You can't stew about whether you should have said something else in a conversation yesterday if you are just paying attention to dribbling down the court.

Practicing mindfulness can decrease your anxiety as well as enrich your life experiences because you are more fully present in everything that you do.

directions

Try each of the following exercises at least once.

Exercise 1

Choose a simple activity that you can do in the next few hours to practice mindfulness. It could be anything from eating a bag of chips to getting dressed to lying on your bed listening to music. Make a conscious effort to perform this activity with mindfulness.

As you perform the actions, try to keep your attention focused only on what you are doing right at that moment. Use all your five senses to experience the activity. Pay close attention to exactly what you are seeing, hearing, feeling, smelling, and tasting as you do this.

Exercise 2

Since we are not used to focusing on the present, it can be hard to keep our minds from wandering. One way to help yourself stay focused is to talk to yourself silently as you perform each activity, simply reminding yourself of what you are doing at the time. For example, as you are eating chips, think to yourself, "Eating, I am eating." As you are getting dressed, think to yourself, "Dressing, I am dressing." It will probably seem a little strange at first, but it will help keep your mind focused on the present and off anxious thoughts.

Exercise 3

As you go through the day, whenever you notice yourself feeling anxious because you have moved your thinking into the future or the past, simply remind yourself, "Come back to the present." Then move your mind away from wherever it has wandered to and bring it back to what you are doing right now.

more to do

Which activity did you choose to practice mindfulness in exercise 1? _____

Describe what you noticed through each of your five senses as you did it.

_____

_____

_____

Describe what it was like for you to try exercise 2. _____

_____

_____

What are the topics you usually think about when your mind moves into the future?

_____

_____

What are the topics you usually think about when your mind moves into the past?

_____

_____

Describe what it was like for you to try exercise 3. _____

_____

_____

Circle how many times you noticed your mind wandering during the day.

once   ten times   hundreds of times   thousands of times

Describe your anxiety level as you tried these exercises. _____

_____

If you are like most people, you will find mindfulness a challenge. Our minds are simply not used to focusing in this way, but with practice, it becomes easier. Tell what it feels like for you to pay attention only to the present moment. _____

_____

_____

28 following your breath

for you to know

Breathing is a natural and effective tool for cultivating peace and decreasing anxiety within you. One way to use your breathing for this purpose is simply to be aware of it.

Our thoughts are the main cause of our anxiety. When our minds are racing from thought to thought, commitment to commitment, fear to fear, they signal our bodies to become tense. Keeping our minds focused on stressful thoughts, or just on too many thoughts at once, can keep our anxiety level high.

Focusing your thoughts on something simple and peaceful will have the opposite effect, and your breath is an ideal point of focus. Left to its natural rhythm, your breath will settle into a very peaceful cadence. It will be balanced and regular, slow and deep—much like it is when you are in a peaceful sleep.

Focusing on your breath is a simple way to bring yourself out of an anxious state and back to peace. It is a tool you always carry with you, so it can be used in any situation, at any time of night or day, wherever you are, whoever you are with, whatever you are doing. You can stop and focus on your breath when you feel yourself getting anxious because you are having an argument with your friend, having a hard time understanding a math problem, getting ready for a job interview, talking with someone you are attracted to, or at any other time.

Putting your attention on your breath for just a minute or two during a time of high anxiety can help you to lower the anxiety and bring yourself back to a peaceful state. Focusing on your breath takes your mind off anxious thoughts and causes your breath to slow and deepen, bringing more oxygen to your body and relaxing it, bringing more oxygen to your mind and clearing it.

directions

Try this exercise to learn how to focus on your breath.

Sit comfortably and close your eyes. Then simply put your attention on your breath. Notice where you feel it. Can you feel air moving in and out of your nostrils? Do you notice it raising and lowering your chest? Does your breath move all the way down into your abdomen when you inhale, or does it move only into your mouth or throat? You don't have to try to change your breathing or make your breath do anything special: your goal is just to find it and follow it and see how it moves as it flows in and out of your body. Continue to follow it for a couple of minutes or for as long as you are comfortable.

Since we are not usually used to paying attention to our breath, this exercise may not come easily at first. Some people say they cannot even locate their breath. If that happens to you, try holding your breath for a few seconds and then releasing it. Stopping breathing and then starting again can make the presence of your breath more obvious to you.

You may have to practice this exercise a few times until it becomes easy to find and follow your breath. Once you can do it more easily, you will not have to close your eyes anymore. You will be able to focus on your breath while you are in class, at a party, in the shower, or eating dinner with your family. If you feel anxious, simply remembering to find your breath and put your attention on it will cause you to slow down and breathe more deeply and will lower your anxiety.

more to do

Over the next day or two, practice paying attention to your breath at different times. Describe how fast or slow, shallow or deep, your breathing is when you are

_____ eating lunch   _____ talking on the phone

_____ in a hard class   _____ riding in the car

_____ in an easy class   _____ listening to music

_____ watching TV   _____ doing homework

_____ hanging out with your friends

Name some situations in which it would be easy for you to focus on your breath without anyone noticing what you are doing.

_____

_____

_____

Name some situations in which it might be harder to focus on your breath without anyone noticing what you are doing.

_____

_____

_____

Name any anxious situations in which it could be helpful for you to focus on your breath.

_____

_____

_____

Describe what happens to your anxiety level as you pay attention to your breath.

_____

_____

_____

29 deep breathing

for you to know

When people are anxious, their breath tends to be shallow and rapid. Making a conscious attempt to breathe more deeply can help you relieve anxiety.

If you watch newborn babies breathe, you will notice that their stomachs rise and fall with each breath. That is because they are naturally breathing deeply and carrying their breath all the way down into their diaphragms. Babies have not yet learned to be stressed. As adults, we tend to inhale our breath into our nostrils, our throats, and sometimes down into our lungs. But rarely do we breathe so deeply that our abdomens move in and out. Most often, our anxious thoughts and hurried activities cause us to breathe using only the upper parts of our respiratory systems. Sometimes, when we are very stressed or in a rush, we may even hold our breath intermittently without realizing it.

Deeper breathing helps relieve anxiety by slowing down our heart rates, relaxing our muscles, and bringing more oxygen deep into our bodies and brains, nourishing our cells more completely and helping us think more clearly. When we are breathing deeply, we are physically less tense. We are also better able to remind ourselves to use positive and rational thinking skills instead of anxiety-producing self-messages and distorted thinking.

directions

Before trying this breathing exercise, it is recommended that you complete Activity 28: Following Your Breath, which will give you practice in finding and following your breath.

Sit or lie down comfortably. Close your eyes so that you can better concentrate and block out distractions. Place your hand gently over your abdomen. Pretend that there is a round balloon in your abdomen, with the opening at the top, or closest to your lungs. Now inhale, and think about pulling your breath all the way down through your body, through the balloon opening and to the bottom of the balloon. As you inhale, let your abdomen rise to make room for your breath. Think about using this breath to fill your body with fresh air, filling the bottom of the balloon first, then the top, then completely filling your lungs from the bottom up.

When you are ready to exhale, gently press down on the bottom of your "balloon" and push the air out of your body from the bottom up, emptying the balloon first, then your lungs and chest.

Repeat this pattern slowly for several minutes, or until it starts to feel comfortable.

Breathing in this way may seem awkward at first. Some people even become anxious because they feel they cannot do it "right." Understand that it is normal to start out feeling this way. It is something new that your body and mind aren't used to. The more you do it, however, the more familiar it will become and the more you will be able to relax. Try to take your time and know that eventually you will get the hang of it. Don't set yourself up for feeling anxious by trying to do it perfectly.

more to do

Circle any of the following things that you noticed while you tried the breathing exercise:

breathing got deeper	muscles twitched
felt awkward	felt stiff
heart rate slowed down	mind wandered
felt peaceful	let go of tension
felt a little anxious	felt sleepy
muscles relaxed	breathing got steadier

other _____

Following is a list of situations in which people can use deep breathing to help them relieve anxiety. Circle those that have happened or might happen to you:

giving an oral report in class	getting a lecture from your parents
taking a test	going through a haunted house
performing in a recital	performing in athletics
going on a job interview	having a tense conversation with a friend
taking your driver's test	doing something new for the first time
going on a date	jumping or diving off the high-dive board

Now make a list of personal situations in your own life in which you could use deep breathing to help you relieve anxiety.

_____

_____

_____

_____

for you to know

Our bodies cannot think for themselves; they only respond to what our brains tell them. If you tell yourself you are in an anxious situation, your body will become tense. If you tell yourself you are in a peaceful situation, your body will become relaxed. Visualizing a peaceful situation in your mind, even if it is not really happening, can help you release anxiety.

At gymnastic meets, Kara used to get anxious as she sat and waited for her turn. To help herself stay peaceful, she learned to use the time to pretend she was sitting in one of her favorite places—in a lawn chair next to the pool at her aunt's house. As Kara waited for the coach to call her to perform, she would picture herself relaxing in the sun, sipping a cool drink. When she replaced her thoughts of anxiety with this mental image of peacefulness, her body responded by relaxing. When her name was finally called, Kara was able to do her gymnastics routine with more grace and confidence because she was working from a state of peace rather than anxiety.

directions

Before starting this exercise, rate your anxiety level on a scale from 0 to 10 (0 being completely peaceful, 10 being highly anxious.) Write your number here: _____

In the space below, draw a picture of the most beautiful, peaceful place you can imagine. It may be a real place or one that just exists in your mind.

To continue this exercise, first read through the text below. You may choose to simply remember it as you visualize your peaceful place, or you may want to have someone else read it to you slowly. The visualization should take from five to ten minutes to complete.

Find a quiet place to sit comfortably, and close your eyes. Take a few deep, slow breaths. Pretend that you are in the beautiful, peaceful place you have just drawn. As you sit there, look around you at everything you can see. Notice how vivid all of the colors are. Notice how clear the air is and how detailed and exquisite every line and shape and texture looks to you. Notice that everything has a sense of peace about it.

Listen to any sounds that are present in this beautiful place. All the sounds you hear are melodic and pleasing to your ears. The sounds add to the sense of harmony and peace that surrounds you. Notice that any scents in the air are also pleasing. They are the most beautiful fragrances you have ever experienced. They add to the peace and relaxation that you feel all around you and within you. As you inhale, you feel as if you are inhaling beauty and relaxation.

Notice that everything you touch feels good to you. The textures that brush against your hands or legs, the air that caresses your face or skin—everything feels gentle and pleasing. Any flavors you taste are pleasant to you, too.

As you experience this time in this beautiful, peaceful place, you are filled with a strong sense of security, stability, and balance. You feel safe, centered, and grounded. You feel calm and sure of yourself. Every cell in your entire body is immersed in peace.

Sit quietly for a minute, just noticing and enjoying this wonderful feeling of peace. Know that this feeling is within you and is yours anytime you want it. All you have to do is remember it. Now you are going to leave this imaginary place and bring your attention back to the room you are in. But you know that you will not lose the ability to return to the peace of this place anytime that you want to. The peace is always within you.

When you open your eyes, rate your anxiety level again. Write your number here: ____

more to do

Describe what it was like for you to do this exercise.

_____

_____

_____

Tell how you chose this place over any other and why this place is peaceful for you.

_____

_____

_____

Look at your anxiety-level ratings from before the exercise and after the exercise. Tell how your anxiety level was affected by the exercise and why you think that happened.

_____

_____

_____

Sometimes people feel uncomfortable with this exercise because they are not used to closing their eyes and picturing things in their mind. Describe any discomfort you may have felt while you were doing the exercise.

_____

_____

_____

You might want to try this exercise picturing a number of different peaceful places. See which one helps you feel the most peaceful. If you practice this exercise on a regular basis as prevention, your everyday level of anxiety will be lowered. If you find your anxiety level rising at some time during the day, try to take a minute to close your eyes and picture yourself in your peaceful place, bringing your body and mind back to a deep state of relaxation. It can help you to practice intervention when your anxiety level is getting too high.

31 meditation

for you to know

Meditation is an exercise that helps you train your brain to let go of anxiety and come back to a peaceful state. When you practice meditation regularly as a prevention exercise, you will find that you are better able to stay calm in situations that used to make you anxious. You will also have a lower level of anxiety in general.

Jared went to his counselor, Mr. Brent, to try to get some ideas on how to feel less anxious. Mr. Brent suggested that Jared try meditation. When Jared heard the word "meditation," he pictured an elderly, bald, religious man in a long robe sitting cross-legged with his eyes closed on top of a mountain. Jared said, "Oh no; that's not for me."

Mr. Brent said that the picture Jared imagined portrayed a common stereotype about meditation but that it was not completely accurate. While meditation *can* be a spiritual practice, it can also simply be a highly effective exercise to calm the mind.

Mr. Brent explained that the basic practice of meditation involves focusing your attention on something peaceful, and then when your mind wanders, bringing it back to that focus of peace again and again. As you take your thoughts away from anxiety and focus on peace, your body will respond by relaxing and releasing tension. As you continue to practice day after day, your mind will get better and better at letting go of stress and staying centered and calm. This ability will help you all throughout every day, no matter what situation you are in.

At first Jared was very skeptical about trying meditation. He thought that sitting still with his eyes closed would just make him feel more anxious. Mr. Brent said it was normal to feel that way at first, but with practice, Jared would get used to it. He suggested Jared try the exercise in his office first, for just thirty seconds to start. After a few thirty-second tries, they moved up to one minute, and then two and three. After a few weeks, Jared was comfortable meditating for five minutes at a time. Jared was surprised that he actually liked meditation. He liked the fact that while he meditated his whole body would relax and his mind would stop racing. He could let go of all feelings of anxiety and also feel more peaceful for a couple of hours afterward. Mr. Brent explained that the greatest benefits of meditation were cumulative: the more regularly Jared practiced, the more focused he would be, the better able to control his emotions, the more deeply he would sleep, and the easier it would be to let go of anxiety.

directions

To practice meditation, you will need to focus on something peaceful. You can choose a word or a mental picture; you can focus on your breath as it moves in and out of your body; or you can try to simply clear your mind of any thoughts at all and focus on the "blackness" behind your eyes.

To help yourself choose a peaceful word or image, circle any of the words below that bring up a feeling of relaxation within you. Use the blank lines to add your own.

sunset	water	nature	clouds	_____
peace	God	smile	relax	_____
free	one	love	flow	_____
sky	float	calm	sail	_____
summer	sleep	quiet	rest	_____

Choose one of the words you circled to focus on during your first try at meditation, or decide to focus on your breath or the darkness. Then follow the steps below:

- Find a quiet place where you will not be disturbed.
- Sit in a position that is comfortable for you.
- Set a timer for one minute.
- Close your eyes.
- Focus your attention on your chosen object of peace.

As you try to focus, it is normal for your mind to wander. When that happens, simply notice it without judgment, and then bring your focus back to your peaceful object again. Know that it is completely normal for your mind to wander again and again and again. Continue refocusing until the time is up.

The goal for meditation practice is to work up to twenty minutes a day, nearly every day. It will not be possible at first. Let yourself start by doing thirty seconds or one minute every few days. As you become comfortable, build up to five minutes, adding thirty seconds or one minute at a time. Add time and days to your practice as you are able. You may add time easily and quickly, or it may take you a year or more to build up to the goal. It doesn't matter how long it takes you. The benefit is in the continued practice of moving your mind away from anxiety and back to peace.

more to do

What did you know or think about meditation before you read this activity? _____

_____

_____

Describe how trying to meditate affected your anxiety level. _____

_____

_____

Describe anything that you liked about it. _____

_____

_____

Describe anything that you didn't like about it. _____

_____

_____

Many people say that they are too busy to meditate. However, when you take time to meditate, you actually end up having more time in your day; regular meditation helps you stay peaceful, so you waste less time being anxious. It helps to you focus, so you complete tasks in less time. You make fewer mistakes, so you spend less time doing things over again. Meditation helps you let go of irritation, so you spend less time in petty arguments. When you compare the amount of time it takes to meditate with the amount of time you waste on these anxious activities, you realize that when you meditate you come out ahead.

Think about realistic times when you could fit meditation into your day. Morning or evening? Right after school or every night before you start your homework? Right after you brush your teeth? As you practice meditating, experiment with different times and different peaceful words or images. Find the way to meditate that works best for you.

32 a higher power

for you to know

Many people believe that there is a power in the world that is greater than human power. People label this power in different ways depending on their beliefs. If you have a belief in a higher power, you can use this to both prevent and manage feelings of anxiety.

The idea of a higher power is usually connected to the concept of spirituality. Spirit is a nonmaterial part of life that has been described as a life-giving force, consciousness, inner being, or soul. You do not need to belong to a particular religion or belief system to have spiritual beliefs, although religious groups are often where people first learn about spiritual ideas.

Having spiritual beliefs can help people manage anxiety in some of the following ways:

1. Lisette believed that she was protected at all times by a power greater than herself. Reminding herself of that helped her feel less anxious.

2. Dominic believed that a higher power had a plan for his life, so there was a reason for everything that happened—even if he didn't understand it at the time. This belief reduced his anxiety when something happened that was unplanned or that he didn't like.

3. Taylor believed that if she prayed, or communicated with a higher power, she could have an effect on the outcome of a situation that made her anxious.

4. For Kurt, just the quiet act of praying lowered his heart rate, released the tension in his muscles, and helped him feel more peaceful.

directions

Circle any of the words below that sound like they are related to your personal spiritual beliefs or ideas about a higher power:

spirit	soul	gratitude	heart
beauty	divine	God	purpose
love	hope	miracles	connectedness
faith	kindness	universe	heaven
peace	worship	nature	holy
forgiveness	eternity		

In the space below, draw a picture, make a collage, write a poem, or tell about your personal spiritual beliefs or your personal ideas about a higher power. Sometimes people don't know exactly what they believe, and that's okay. If that is the case for you, just express your guesses.

more to do

Tell whether it was easy or difficult for you to describe your ideas about a higher power, and why.

_____

_____

_____

_____

Look at the words and pictures that express your beliefs. Describe any feelings of peace that they bring up in you, and tell why.

_____

_____

_____

_____

Describe any feelings of anxiety that your words and pictures bring up in you, and tell why.

_____

_____

_____

_____

If your beliefs about a higher power raise your anxiety level, it might be helpful for you to share your feelings with an adult with whom you feel comfortable.

Describe a situation that you have been feeling anxious about recently, and tell how you might use belief in a higher power to help you to feel more peaceful.

_____

_____

_____

_____

33 it's a cinch by the inch

for you to know

People can become anxious if they try to think about or do too much at one time. You can lower your anxiety level by breaking a big project down into smaller steps. The saying, "It's a cinch by the inch, but it's hard by the yard" reminds us that tackling something a little at a time makes it easier.

It was 1:00 P.M. and Stephen wanted to go skateboarding with his friends at 2:00 P.M. His mother told him he had to clean his room before he could go. He looked around at the dirty clothes and clean clothes mixed together on the floor, the empty soda cans lined up on his desk, the magazines mixed with homework papers, his unmade bed, and the layer of dust over everything. He thought, "I'll never get this all done" and felt a knot of anxiety beginning in his stomach. His mom came into the room and reminded him, "It's a cinch by the inch. You can't do it all at once. Start with one small task, complete it, and then move on to the next."

Stephen looked around the room again, trying to see a lot of small tasks instead of one big one. He began to relax a little. He saw the soda cans first and carried them down to the kitchen. Then he made his bed. Next he sorted his magazines and homework, put his magazines into the drawer and his homework into his backpack. He saw that his room was looking better already—all he had left were his clothes and dusting. First, he separated the clean clothes from the dirty ones. Then he put his dirty clothes into the hamper. Next he folded his clean clothes and put them away. It was only 1:40 P.M.! He got the dust-cloth, cleaned his desk, dresser, and nightstand, and still had fifteen minutes to spare.

directions

Help Sara use the idea, "It's a cinch by the inch" in the following scenario:

Sara was listening to the teacher assign an English report. When she heard all the work that had to be done, she felt perspiration start to form on her palms, and the muscles in her shoulders begin to tense. The report had to be typed and put into a folder, with a special cover designed to coordinate with the subject. She had to choose a book to read and watch a video about the same story, then compare the two in her report. She also had to turn in an outline of the report and make notecards for an oral presentation. Sara thought she could never get it all done by the end of the semester. Her shoulders got tighter and tighter.

Reread the preceding paragraph and identify all the small steps involved in Sara's big project. Write them separately on the lines below.

_____

_____

_____

_____

Look at the list of steps that make up Sara's project. Close your eyes for a minute and think about having to complete all those steps yourself. Rate your anxiety level about completing the whole project on a 0 to 10 scale (0 being completely peaceful and 10 being highly anxious).

0   1   2   3   4   5   6   7   8   9   10

Now close your eyes again and think about having to complete just one of the steps. Rate your anxiety level about completing this project just one step at a time on the same scale.

0   1   2   3   4   5   6   7   8   9   10

activity 33 * it's a cinch by the inch

Describe any difference between your first and second anxiety ratings. Tell why you think your anxiety level went up, went down, or stayed the same.

_____

_____

_____

_____

more to do

Sometimes the things that make us feel anxious don't even have that many steps. We may be anxious just because they are in areas where we don't have much confidence. For Sara, just the step of typing the report produced anxiety because she wasn't sure of her typing skills. Sara learned that she could break even this task down into small steps: turn on the computer, open up a new file, type the title page first, type one page at a time.

Describe a task you must complete that makes you feel anxious.

_____

_____

_____

_____

Break this task down into small, manageable steps and write them here.

_____

_____

_____

_____

Take one of the steps above and break it down into smaller steps.

_____

_____

_____

_____

activity 33 ✱ it's a cinch by the inch

How does your anxiety level differ when you focus on the whole project versus just one step?

_____

_____

_____

_____

for you to know

People often become anxious when confronted with a situation they think they don't know how to handle. Using problem-solving skills can help you to reduce your feelings of anxiety at these times.

Using problem-solving skills means that instead of becoming overwhelmed or anxious when you encounter a challenging situation, you use your body and mind to help you find a solution. You can remember how to problem solve by using this three-word reminder: Stop, Breathe, and Think.

1. "Stop" means that you have to take a time-out from your initial anxious reaction to the situation. You literally stop whatever you are doing and remain still for a moment. Then, you…

2. "Breathe." Now is the time to take a long, deep breath, moving your mental focus away from anxiety and onto your breathing. It helps your heart rate to slow down and sends necessary oxygen to all parts of your body, releasing tension in your muscles. When you breathe deeply, you receive more oxygen in your brain, which allows you to…

3. "Think" more clearly and effectively. Now you can look at the situation and think carefully about what you need to do first, second, and third, to solve the immediate problem. Once you identify these steps, you can put them into action.

directions

Pretend that you have just encountered each of the situations below. Look at the scene in front of you. Then practice problem solving by following these steps:

1. Close your eyes and *stop* looking at the scene.

2. Take a deep *breath*.

3. *Think* carefully and clearly about what you need to do first, second, and third to help solve the problem.

Write your step-by-step problem-solving plan under the picture.

You are babysitting your younger sister. You walk into the room and see...

_____

_____

_____

_____

You are riding your bike near your house. You turn the corner and see…

You walk into the art room at school and see…

more to do

Some people think problem solving is a skill that would be hard to learn, but most of us problem solve in many ways every day. A few problem-solving activities are listed below. Circle any that you already know how to do. Then write some more of your own.

doing a jigsaw puzzle   organizing friends to go to the movies

planning a party   making your lunch

writing a paper   resolving a disagreement

cleaning your room   burning a CD

_____

_____

_____

No matter how simple they seem, all of these activities involve thinking clearly and making and following a step-by-step plan. Choose two of the activities above and list the problem-solving steps you would use to complete them.

_____

_____

_____

_____

_____

_____

_____

Sometimes people think they would not be able to problem solve if a situation was too unfamiliar or seemed too big for them. Most of us underestimate ourselves in this way. Think back to problems that you have already encountered and solved in the past. These problems might have to do with school, home, relationships, or activities. Make a list of them here.

_____

_____

_____

_____

Describe a situation that happened to you recently in which you were feeling very anxious. Tell what steps your problem-solving plan would have involved if you had been able to stop, breathe, and think.

_____

_____

_____

_____

Sometimes a situation will be so complicated or difficult that you will not be able to handle it by yourself. In those cases, part of your problem-solving plan should be to find someone to help you. Describe a situation that you might encounter in which you would need to ask for help. Tell whom you would find to help you.

_____

_____

_____

_____

35 keeping your life in balance

for you to know

When people keep their lives in balance, their anxiety level tends to be lower. Staying in balance means that the way you choose to spend your time and energy is a healthy mix of leisure and responsibilities.

Rachel, Jennifer, and Stephanie were the same age, lived in the same neighborhood, went to the same school, and were in the same grade. But Rachel and Jennifer were usually anxious, while Stephanie was relaxed.

Rachel spent most of her time rushing from one activity to the next. Along with school, she was in the band, took flute lessons, was on the track and lacrosse teams, had a part-time job walking dogs, and volunteered at a senior citizens' home. She also did her homework and household chores and helped with her mom's home business. She was almost always anxious about getting everything done. Rachel's life was out of balance and brought on anxiety because she tried to do too much for the amount of time she had.

Jennifer was in only one activity, Junior Achievement Club. She spent all of the rest of her time after school and on the weekends studying and doing homework. She felt like she had to study all the time to get the best possible grades so she could go to a good college. She was usually very anxious about whether she was studying hard enough. Jennifer's life was out of balance and brought on anxiety because she spent all of her time working and no time on leisure activities.

Stephanie spent her time with three main activities: she took violin lessons, played soccer, and did her homework. She also spent time with her family and friends, going bowling, to the movies, and camping. Stephanie enjoyed everything she did and rarely felt anxious or overwhelmed. Stephanie's life was in balance because she did a moderate number of activities and balanced work with play.

directions

On the scales below, record approximately how much time you spend on your responsibilities and your leisure activities over the next two days.

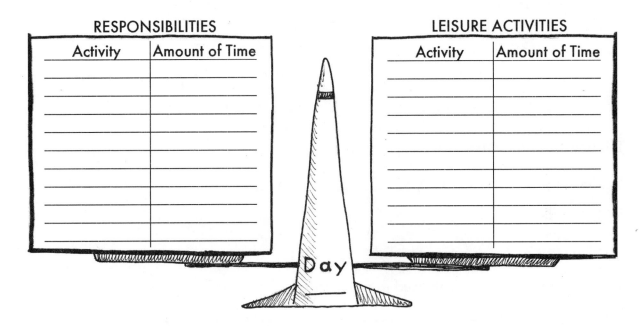

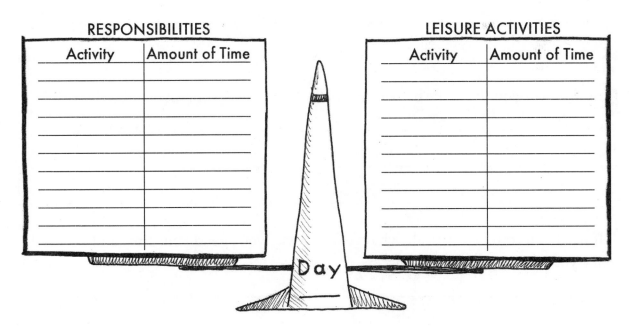

more to do

Look back at the pictures of your scales. Describe anything you notice about the balance of your life.

_____

_____

_____

Tell how your daily balance compares to

Rachel's _____

Jennifer's _____

Stephanie's _____

Tell why your scales are balanced or unbalanced.

_____

_____

_____

Describe how you think the balance of your scales affects your anxiety level.

_____

_____

_____

Tell what you could realistically change in the way you spend your time and energy to make your scales more balanced.

_____

_____

_____

for you to know

Keeping your environment in order can help you to find things that you need more easily and quickly. That can help to keep your anxiety level lower.

Peter was often anxious because he couldn't find the things he needed. He carried his backpack from class to class, but it was such a mess inside that he couldn't always find his homework, assignment book, or pencils when he needed them. Then he became anxious. He wouldn't be able to participate in class, and his teacher would be upset with him because he wasn't prepared.

Peter kept all his school belongings in his locker, but it was such a mess that he couldn't always find his gym shorts, library books, or class notebooks when he needed them. Then he became anxious. Searching for his belongings would make him late for class, he wouldn't be able to participate, and his teacher would take points off because he wasn't prepared.

Peter had all his personal belongings in his bedroom at home: clothes, video games, sports equipment, computer supplies, and materials he needed for his music lessons. But his room was such a mess that he couldn't always find his basketball jersey, his extra guitar strings, the disks with his English reports, or his good shoes when he needed them. Then he became anxious. He would be late for his appointments, he wouldn't be able to participate, and people would be upset with him because he wasn't prepared.

Peter's older sister, Michelle, was almost always organized, and she was rarely anxious about finding things. She told Peter that it would help him to learn about categories.

If he could learn to put things into categories on a regular basis, he would be far more organized and far less anxious. Michelle said that categories are just groups of things that have something in common with each other. She helped Peter organize the things in his room by category, and then Peter did the same thing with his backpack and locker. He was able to find things more easily and quickly, and that eliminated a lot of his anxiety.

directions

Go to any store near you. Each store has many products. If they weren't organized by category, things would be a mess and it would be hard to find what you were looking for. Draw a picture or write about how you see things categorized in the store.

Go to your local library or your school library. Each library has many books and many different kinds of books. If they weren't organized by category, things would be a mess and it would be hard to find what you were looking for. On the next page, draw a picture or write about how you see things categorized in the library.

Sit in the doorway of your bedroom and look around you. You have a lot of belongings in your bedroom. When things aren't organized by category, it can be a mess and hard to find what you are looking for. Draw a picture or write about how you can categorize the things in your room.

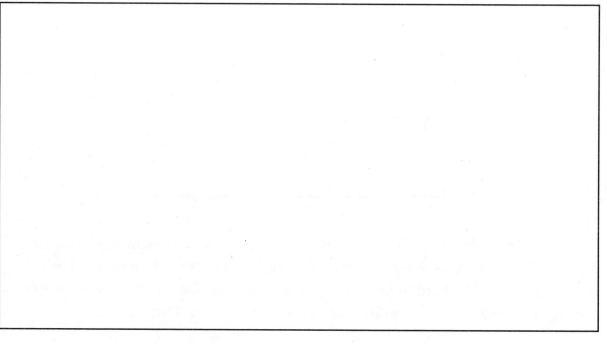

more to do

Describe a time when being unorganized caused you to feel anxious.

_____

_____

What changes could you make so that wouldn't happen again?

_____

_____

In your room, which categories are the most important for you to keep organized, and why?

_____

_____

Describe other places that you need to be organized, and tell why.

_____

_____

_____

One of the tricks to being organized is *staying* organized. Organizing your belongings once is just the beginning. Then you have to learn to keep them organized. Imagine you just finished organizing your room on Sunday night. On Monday afternoon, your mom gave you your clean laundry to put away, you brought two finished art projects and three homework assignments home from school, and you had to dump your backpack out on your floor to find your lab partner's phone number. Describe what you would have to do and when you would have to do it to keep your room organized.

_____

_____

_____

37 managing your time

for you to know

Not having enough time to do things and always being late are habits that can raise your anxiety level. When you can learn to manage your time appropriately, it is easier to stay peaceful.

Marissa was frequently anxious because she was running late for things. She was in the pep club, student council, soccer, and the ecology club. She also babysat and taught Sunday school. At home she was responsible for cleaning her room, vacuuming, and taking out the recycling. She had so many activities that she had to stay up very late to get all her homework done. That made it hard for her to wake up in the morning, so she was often late for school. After she had had three detentions for being late to her first class, the assistant principal, Ms. Barnes, called Marissa into her office. They had a talk about Marissa's situation, and Ms. Barnes said that Marissa needed to learn how to manage her time better. She taught Marissa the following four steps for time management:

Step 1: Scheduling
Before you make plans or take on another activity or responsibility, check your schedule. See what else you are doing that day. Do you have time to do another activity? Commit to only as much as you have time for.

Step 2: Recording
Choose a scheduling tool in which you will record everything that you have to do. Some scheduling tools include calendars, electronic organizers, day planner books, or assignment books. Always check your schedule before you make a plan, and as soon as you schedule something, record it.

Step 3: Checking

Every morning when you first get up, check your schedule to see what you have to do that day. If you need extra help remembering, write yourself reminder notes and leave them where you will see them. Every time you think about making a commitment to do something, check your schedule to see if you have enough time. Check your schedule throughout the day to make sure you are remembering your commitments.

Step 4: Planning Ahead

Think ahead. Don't wait until the last minute to do things. Make sure you allow yourself enough time for each task or commitment.

The next day, Marissa tried the four-step plan. When her friend Becca asked her to go to the movies that night, Marissa's first thought was to say yes. But then she got out her day planner. She saw that she already had a student council meeting and she had to study for a math test that night. Then she looked ahead two days and saw that Friday evening was free. She and Becca decided to go to the movies on Friday instead. Marissa wrote it in her planner right away. She also made a note to come home right after soccer practice on Friday instead of stopping for pizza with the team like she usually did. She realized that if she went out for pizza, she wouldn't have time to shower and change and be ready to go to the movie when Becca picked her up. Just to make sure she didn't forget, she wrote herself a note and put it in the duffel bag she always took to soccer practice. Marissa felt her anxiety level drop already, just knowing that she wouldn't have to rush around.

directions

Make seven copies of the planning page below. For the next week, practice scheduling all of your commitments, from test dates to after-school activities to chores.

Day _____	Date _____
5 A.M.	
6 A.M.	
7 A.M.	
8 A.M.	
9 A.M.	
10 A.M.	
11 A.M.	
12 noon	
1 P.M.	
2 P.M.	
3 P.M.	
4 P.M.	
5 P.M.	
6 P.M.	
7 P.M.	
8 P.M.	
9 P.M.	
10 P.M.	
11 P.M.	
12 midnight	

more to do

Describe what it was like for you to keep the planning pages.

_____

_____

_____

Tell how keeping the planning pages affected your anxiety level.

_____

_____

_____

Which of the four time-management steps is the easiest for you to accomplish, and why?

_____

_____

_____

Which of the four time-management steps do you need the most help with, and why?

_____

_____

_____

Describe what you could do to help yourself achieve the step that is hardest for you.

_____

_____

_____

Tell which scheduling tool works the best for you, and why.

_____

_____

_____

unexpressed anger 38

for you to know

When people feel angry, they carry their anger with them until it is expressed—directly, indirectly, verbally, or physically. When anger is expressed, it dissipates. Anger that is not recognized or expressed doesn't just disappear. It is still carried in your body and emotions and may appear later as a feeling of anxiety. Exploring your experiences with anger may help you to relieve anxiety.

People learn to deal with anger in different ways. In Cate's family, anger was expressed by shouting and breaking things. It made Cate very uncomfortable, and she tended to either ignore her feelings of anger or hold them in.

In Evan's family, people were encouraged to take their anger outside to the basketball hoop or to the treadmill in the basement. Evan learned to let his anger out when he played sports at school.

In Vanessa's family, no one showed anger. They kept their feelings to themselves. Vanessa wasn't sure what to do when she was angry. Usually she wrote about it in her diary, and sometimes she cried.

Anger should be expressed in safe ways, such as appropriate verbal expression, physical activity or exercise, writing, drawing, or playing music. When you practice paying attention to your feelings of anger and expressing them safely and completely, you may find that your anxiety level decreases.

activity 38 ✳ unexpressed anger

directions

On the line in each space below, write the names of things, people, or situations that make you angry. For each item, color in the mercury of the thermometer on the left to show the level of your anger and color in the mercury of the thermometer on the right to show the amount of anger that you express about it.

If you don't think that anything makes you angry, ask yourself, "If something did make me angry, what would it be?" Then fill in the spaces and thermometers according to your answer.

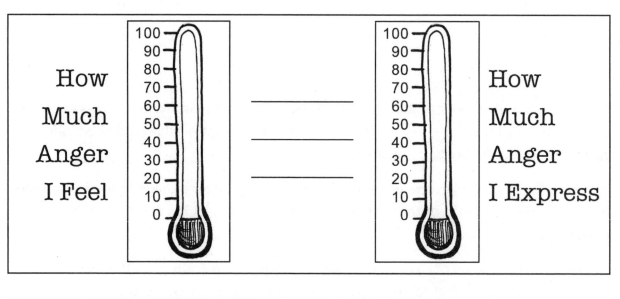

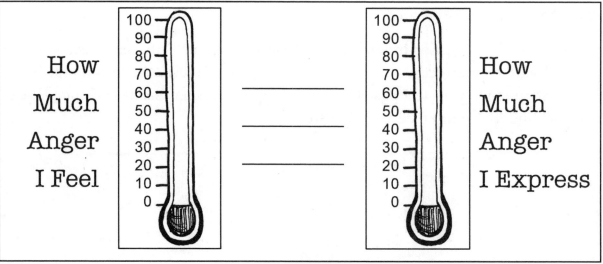

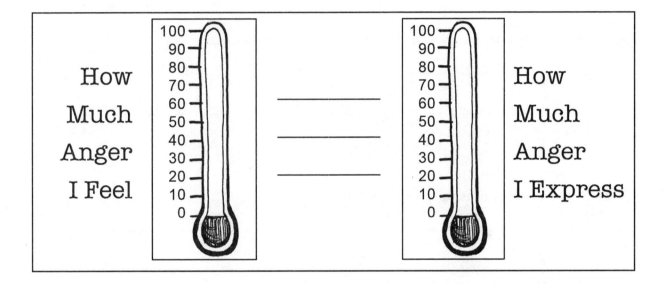

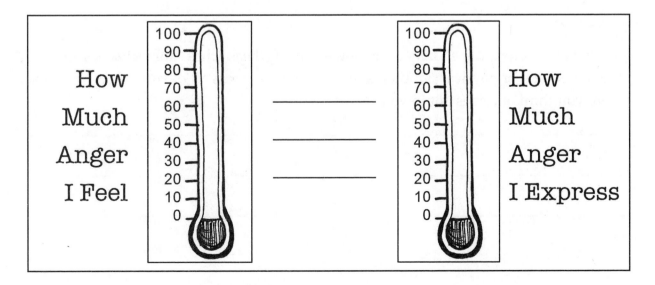

more to do

Describe how the amount of anger you feel about each item compares to the amount of anger you express.

_____

_____

_____

Describe the ways people in your family usually express anger.

_____

_____

_____

Describe the ways you usually express anger.

_____

_____

_____

Anger that is not expressed may come out as anxiety, headaches, stomachaches, or other emotional or physical symptoms. If you do not express all of your anger, describe where you think it comes out in you.

_____

_____

_____

Tell what else you could do to let out anger that may not be expressed.

_____

_____

_____

Describe anything that comes to mind that you could be angry about and may not even realize.

_____

_____

_____

39 managing fears and phobias

for you to know

A phobia is a strong, persistent fear of a specific object or situation that causes anxiety to rise quickly when one is exposed to it. Some common phobias are claustrophobia, or fear of closed spaces; acrophobia, or fear of heights; agoraphobia, or fear of crowded public places; aviophobia, or fear of flying; and hemophobia, or fear of blood. People usually try to manage phobias by simply avoiding the object or situation that causes the anxiety. Phobias can also be reduced or completely eliminated by using a technique called systematic desensitization.

Haley was apprehensive about her commitment to be a junior counselor at summer camp. As much as she wanted to help with the younger girls, swim, sail, and do crafts, she didn't know if she could handle her extreme fear of spiders. Last year at camp, a spider had gotten into Haley's suitcase and into her T-shirt. When she put the shirt on, the spider had crawled onto her bare skin, and she screamed. Haley had been so upset she had left camp two days early.

Her mother made an appointment for Haley to see a counselor who specialized in helping people with anxiety, fears, and phobias. The counselor told Haley she could help her, using systematic desensitization. It was a technique that could help her feel peaceful instead of fearful when she thought about or encountered spiders. First, Haley had to make a list of situations with spiders that made her feel afraid. Next, she had to put them in order of how strong the fear was. The counselor called this list a "hierarchy." Haley's hierarchy looked like this:

Least fearful to most fearful situations with spiders

A spider crawling outside my tent

A spider crawling inside my tent

A spider crawling near my cot

A spider crawling on my cot

A spider crawling on me on top of my clothes

A spider crawling on my bare skin

A spider crawling near or on my face

At the next session, the counselor had Haley sit comfortably, close her eyes, and rate her anxiety level on a 0 to 10 scale, 0 being completely peaceful and 10 being highly anxious. Haley said it was at a 5. The counselor helped Haley relax all of her muscles one by one. Then she had Haley visualize a very safe and peaceful place in her mind. Haley's anxiety level went down to 0. Then the counselor told her to picture a spider crawling outside her tent. Her anxiety level rose to 3. Haley relaxed her muscles and pictured her safe, peaceful place again. She continued to focus on relaxing until she could picture the spider outside her tent and keep her anxiety at a 1. Then she moved on to the next situation, a spider crawling inside her tent.

Haley continued to go back and forth between relaxing and visualizing the spider. She had to repeat the exercise a number of times over the course of a few counseling sessions, but eventually Haley was able to picture a spider crawling near her face and keep her anxiety level at a 1. Haley kept practicing the exercise at home and soon became confident that she could go to camp again.

directions

Planning and carrying out a systematic desensitization exercise is often done best with the help of another person. Think of someone with whom you feel comfortable talking about it, and if possible, ask that person to help you complete this exercise.

Draw a picture or write about your fear or phobia in the box below.

Write your own hierarchy of statements about the fear or phobia.

_____

_____

_____

_____

_____

_____

_____

_____

Read through the format of Haley's systematic desensitization exercise again to familiarize yourself with the process. Then follow the same steps that she did, moving between deep relaxation and visualizing the feared object or situation until you can comfortably visualize each step on your hierarchy without your anxiety level rising too high.

As you practice, you may find that you will want to revise your hierarchy at least once. It is common to make the steps too big or too general at first. Identifying smaller steps will help the exercise to be more effective.

more to do

Tell why you think you developed a fear of this particular object or situation.

_____

_____

_____

Describe what it was like for you to go through the relaxation part of this exercise.

_____

_____

_____

Tell what might help you to relax even more.

_____

_____

_____

Describe what it was like for you to visualize your fear or phobia.

_____

_____

_____

Which step on your hierarchy was the hardest to relax with?

_____

_____

_____

Which step was the easiest to relax with?

_____

_____

_____

Tell how your life might be different if you could overcome this fear.

_____

_____

_____

Remember that you may have to do this exercise a number of times before you find your fear diminishing. Be patient with yourself and realize that is normal.

40 managing panic

for you to know

A panic attack is a short period of very intense anxiety that causes much discomfort. People can learn to manage panic attacks by following some simple guidelines. If you have panic attacks regularly, you should be sure to tell an adult and also your doctor.

Tony had his first panic attack when he was visiting his mother in the hospital. His mom had just had surgery to remove a tumor. As Tony walked into the room and saw his mother asleep in the hospital bed, looking pale and with tubes in her arms, he felt himself becoming light-headed. His heart began to pound, and his stomach was queasy. He began to perspire, and it felt like his arms were tingling. Tony's father noticed that something was wrong. He had Tony sit down in a chair and he called a nurse. The nurse told Tony to take long, deep breaths, which he did for a few minutes, until the feeling subsided. He soon felt better but was shaken up by what had happened. The physical discomfort had come on so fast that it scared him. He didn't know why it had happened and was afraid it might happen again. The next day, Tony was nervous about going to school, but his father said he had to. Tony felt himself worrying all morning, and during his lunch break he went to the school nurse's office.

When Tony told the school nurse what had happened the day before, she said it sounded like he had experienced a panic attack. She told him that people may have panic attacks when they are under strong stress, and seeing his mother looking frail and weak in the hospital could certainly trigger stress. She told Tony that panic attacks are not dangerous and can be handled very simply. Finally, she gave Tony a printed handout with a list of things he could do if he ever felt that way again. Tony felt better knowing that there was a name for what had happened and that he could manage it if it happened again.

The handout the school nurse gave him read as follows:

Using Your Mind and Body to Manage Panic Attacks

Using Your Mind

1. Remind yourself that you are not in danger. You are just having an exaggerated experience of a normal reaction to stress.

2. Remind yourself that you can manage the uncomfortable feelings.

3. Instead of thinking thoughts like, "Oh my gosh, this is awful! What's going to happen to me?" think, "Okay, I recognize these feelings. I know exactly what to do to release them, and I'll do it now."

Using Your Body

1. Find a place where you can sit down. If you are outside, lean against something solid.

2. Begin to slow your breathing by taking long, deep breaths. Remember that breathing deeply will bring the needed oxygen back into your body, stop your heart from racing, and eliminate any tingling or dizzy feelings.

3. Look around and notice all the normal things going on around you. Focus on that normalcy as you allow the fearful symptoms to pass.

4. To relieve your symptoms, do other things that feel comforting to you. Some people sip cool water, some lie down and close their eyes, and some put a cool cloth on the base of their neck.

---

directions

Circle any of the symptoms below that you have experienced during a panic attack:

pounding heart	chest pains	sweating
light-headedness	nausea	tingling
numbness	fear of dying	dizziness
stomach problems	chills	flushes
shortness of breath	shaking	feeling of unreality
feeling out of control	feeling of smothering	feeling of choking

In the space below, draw a picture of yourself calmly managing your panic symptoms. Use detail to show the comfortable position you are in, the relaxation of your muscles and breathing, and the clarity of your mind. Add a thought balloon, and write in the peaceful, reassuring, confident thoughts you are thinking to relieve your feelings of panic.

more to do

Describe what happened the last time you had a panic attack.

_____

_____

_____

_____

Tell the things you thought or did that made the symptoms worse.

_____

_____

_____

_____

Tell the things you thought or did that made the symptoms diminish.

_____

_____

_____

_____

If you have had more than one panic attack, list the times of day, days of the week, and circumstances under which the panic attacks occurred, as best you can remember.

_____

_____

_____

_____

Do you notice any patterns in the information you have listed?

_____

_____

_____

_____

If you have panic attacks regularly, keep a diary of their characteristics for the next five to ten times you have them. Describe any patterns you see in the information.

_____

_____

_____

_____

Tell how you can use this information to avoid panic attacks in the future.

_____

_____

_____

_____

Look back at the picture you drew of yourself peacefully managing the panic. As you look at it, breathe deeply and really create the feeling of peacefulness in your body. Close your eyes and picture yourself in your drawing, calmly handling the panic. Know that you can do this whenever you need to.

separating yourself from other people's problems 41

for you to know

Sometimes it is hard to keep from feeling anxious when people you know or love are feeling anxious. But taking on other people's problems only raises your own anxiety even higher and makes you more vulnerable to becoming overwhelmed.

Jasmine had a very close group of friends. They were in a lot of the same classes and went to movies together almost every weekend. Jasmine was a caring person and a good listener, so her friends often came to her with their problems. Jasmine always felt good when she could help them by giving advice or just sympathizing, but sometimes she felt herself worrying about her friends' problems for hours afterward. When she did that, she would get a kind of prickly, burning feeling across the top of her back and shoulders. She told her mom about it, and her mom said they should have the doctor check it out.

After listening to her story and examining her, the doctor told Jasmine that the feeling was most likely connected to her nerves. When she got too anxious, her nerves got "overloaded." It was a common stress reaction. He said that Jasmine needed to learn to let go of her friends' problems. She didn't have to stop listening or being a good friend; she just had to stop holding their problems within her.

The doctor gave Jasmine some suggestions for how to do this:

1. Remind herself about the worthlessness of worry.

2. When she is not with her friends and is still thinking about their problems, practice thought stopping.

3. When she is listening to her friends' problems, picture herself with a special invisible shield around her. Love and caring can go out from her through the shield, but stress from their problems is blocked from coming in.

4. Practice visualizing leaving her friends' problems with them. After she has listened to her friends and is walking away from them, she can picture herself walking away from the problems, too. For example, she might picture the problems as little gremlins standing at her friends' feet or sitting on their shoulders. Or when she hangs up the phone after talking to a friend, she can picture the problems physically trapped within the phone line, so that when she hangs up, they stay in there and do not come with her.

5. Remind herself that caring about someone and taking on their problems are two different things. Taking on someone else's worries doesn't help them; it just drains her of energy that she could be using to be a good listener or for staying healthy in her own life.

Jasmine tried some of the doctor's suggestions. At first it was hard to separate herself from her friends' problems, but eventually she got better at it, and the burning in her shoulders went away. She realized she could be an even better friend if she wasn't overly stressed.

directions

Think of a situation in which you feel anxious about someone else's problems. In the space below, draw a picture of yourself and that person. Draw your heart to symbolize your caring for them. Then use lines, colors, or shapes to show the anxiety that surrounds the two of you.

Draw another picture of yourself and that person when you have separated yourself from the problems. Again draw your heart to symbolize your caring, but this time, use lines, colors, or shapes to show that the anxiety is a good distance away from you. Draw a heavy line or barrier between yourself and the anxiety.

more to do

Describe how you feel in the first picture.

_____

Does your feeling anxious help the other person at all? ☐ Yes ☐ No

Describe how you feel in the second picture.

_____

Does your not feeling anxious hurt the other person in any way? ☐ Yes ☐ No

_____

_____

_____

Look at your heart in both pictures. How do you think feeling the other person's anxiety affects your ability to care about them?

_____

_____

_____

The next time you feel anxious about someone else's problem, try one of the suggestions Jasmine's doctor gave her. Describe your experience here.

_____

_____

_____

Continue to try the suggestions on Jasmine's list until you find one that works well for you. Or think of your own idea for separating yourself from other people's anxiety. Describe it here and then try it out.

_____

_____

_____

_____

_____

_____

_____

42 future challenges

for you to know

By working through the exercises in this book, you may have learned a number of ways to successfully manage your feelings of anxiety. While it does not mean that you will never experience anxiety again, it does mean that you have gained valuable coping skills to help you move through your life more peacefully.

Learning ways to cope with anxiety means that an important change has taken place inside of you. You have learned new ways of thinking and behaving that can help you keep feelings of anxiety at a lower level, no matter where you go or what you do for the rest of your life.

Sometimes people think that because they have learned these coping skills, they should never feel anxious again. If they do experience anxiety, they tell themselves that they must have done something wrong, and they become more anxious, upset, frustrated, or depressed. They feel like they have failed at managing anxiety.

It is important to remember that managing anxiety and eliminating anxiety are two different things. Coping skills help you to take care of yourself and keep anxiety from getting too high. But using coping skills does not mean that you will never feel anxious again. There will always be new situations and new challenges in your life. Expecting to eliminate anxiety completely is unrealistic. Thinking this way will set you up to feel like a failure because it is something that is nearly impossible to achieve.

Expecting to use healthy coping skills to keep your daily anxiety level lower and manage higher anxiety when it comes along is a goal that you can achieve. The more you continue to practice managing anxiety through prevention and intervention, the more easily and quickly you will handle new situations when they arise. But keep in mind that you will continue to be presented with new challenges that bring up anxiety for the rest of your life. That does not mean that you have failed; it just means that you are human and alive.

activity 42 ✳ future challenges

directions

Write the current year at the far left end of the timeline below. At the markers that follow, write what the year will be one year, two years, five years, and ten years from now.

Inside the first marker, make a list of the challenges that you face in your life today. In the markers that follow, make a list of possible challenges that you might face at each of those dates in the future.

more to do

Tell which anxiety-management techniques you have learned in this book that you think will be helpful to you at the present time.

_____

_____

_____

Tell which anxiety-management techniques you think will be most helpful to you in the future, and why.

_____

_____

_____

Which anxiety-management techniques might you like to learn more about, and why?

_____

_____

_____

This workbook may have taught you some important skills, but it is just a beginning. There are many other books, workbooks, classes, and teachers that you can continue to learn from. Which method is the easiest way for you to learn, and why?

_____

_____

_____

activity 42 * future challenges

You have accomplished a lot by working through this book. You have spent time and energy on learning how to help yourself, and that is one of the most valuable investments you can make. It will affect your ability to handle everything else in your life. Congratulate yourself for your work! Then share your accomplishment by telling someone else what you have done.

Lisa M. Schab, LCSW, is a licensed clinical social worker with a private counseling practice in the Chicago suburbs. She writes a monthly parenting column for *Chicago Parent* magazine and is the author of eight self-help books and workbooks for children and adults. Schab teaches self-help and relaxation therapy workshops for the general public and professional training courses for therapists. She received her bachelor's degree from Northwestern University and her master's degree in clinical social work from Loyola University.